INDIVISIBLE

INDIVISIBLE

How to Forge Our Differences into a Stronger Future

DENISE HAMILTON

Countryman Press

An Imprint of W. W. Norton & Company
Independent Publishers Since 1923

INDIVISIBLE is a work of nonfiction. Individual names and potentially identifying details have been altered in certain cases, and some incidents and accounts are composites.

For information about permission to reproduce selections from this book, write to Permissions, Countryman Press, 500 Fifth Avenue, New York, NY 10110

For information about special discounts for bulk purchases, please contact W. W. Norton Special Sales at specialsales@wwnorton.com or 800-233-4830

Manufacturing by Lake Book Manufacturing
Production manager: Devon Zahn

Countryman Press
www.countrymanpress.com

An imprint of W. W. Norton & Company, Inc.
500 Fifth Avenue, New York, NY 10110
www.wwnorton.com

978-1-68268-838-0

10 9 8 7 6 5 4 3 2 1

To Matt and Javan, my Indivisible Team.

CONTENTS

Prologue

What Does It Mean to Be Indivisible?

A FEW YEARS AGO, I WAS SCROLLING MINDLESSLY THROUGH MY phone when I saw a statistic about the maternal mortality rate in the United States. Black women were dying in childbirth at three times the rate of White women.[1] According to a 2021 report from the CDC, the national average maternal mortality rate for Black women is 48.9 deaths per 100,000 live births, compared to 14.7 deaths per 100,000 live births for White women.[2] Not because they were in rural areas or having their babies at home. Not because they weren't vocal about needing medical attention or didn't have money for proper care. Serena Williams nearly died because her doctors initially dismissed her concerns that she was short of breath. She insisted she needed to be examined, and the doctors found blood clots in her lungs.[3] Black women were in the same hospitals, with the same doctors; they just weren't receiving the same treatment. At a time when these women were most vulnerable, they were dying. Dying from difference.

I was furious. Apoplectic, actually. I remembered the terrifying experience of giving birth to my daughter and, as a Black woman myself, I was enraged at the deep tragedy of having to manage both contractions and racism. I didn't die. I consider myself lucky, but I shouldn't have to be lucky to survive. None of us should.

The next day, I came across another objectively horrifying statistic: The suicide rate among White men in America is one of the highest in the world.[4] And I felt nothing.

I didn't care. I didn't care at all.

In my experience, White men had everything. They were society's winners. They got the good jobs and the nice houses, and they didn't care about me. As a Black woman, my whole life had been spent navigating their rules and battling their countless arbitrary advantages. From my vantage point, they had every opportunity, and their wealth, power, and success were usually derived at the expense of people who look like me. Why do they need me to worry about them? Who cares what their struggles are?

My sleep was fitful that night. I got up the next morning, tired and shaken by my deep hypocrisy. Like so many of us, I'd told myself the story that I was a good person: kind, understanding, and inclusive. But when confronted with an actual situation that challenged my beloved story of the world, was I?

That morning was the beginning of a necessary process of exploration for me. How did I get here? What did it mean to be human? How were we all connected? What is our responsibility to each other?

I began to read articles and watch documentaries about this suicide scourge among White men. I learned about the factors that were causing them to take their own lives so much more often than the rest of the American population. I read about the loneliness epidemic, the isolation, and the loss of community. I began to understand the part unfettered access to guns played in this battle. Most gun deaths in the United States are suicides, and White men, despite the narrative you hear on the news, are far more likely to own a gun, even multiple guns, than Black or Hispanic men.[5]

I learned about the socialization of White males toward stoicism, secrecy, and avoidance of mental health care professionals.[6] I was confronted by a perverse tragedy. White men are born with advantages conferred by race and gender, but commitment to the mythology of their superiority was a trap. Loss of a job, failure of a business, loneliness, and underemployment; every group experiences these things. But for some White men, losing status could be a death sentence.

While I, as a Black woman, have been plagued my whole life by the cruel violence of low expectations, I had never really considered the converse: That some White men are literally being crushed by failure in the face of idealized expectations. I had always felt suffocated by the mask the world expected me to wear, but I came to learn that White men could be strangled by their masks as well. I started to see why, although White men are 30 percent of the population, they account for 70 percent of the suicides.[7]

As an inclusion strategist, my days are spent helping others unpack their preconceived notions and reimagining an inclusive world. I am a Black woman who emigrated from Jamaica as a small child, grew up in Brooklyn, New York, and attended predominantly Black schools, White Schools, and Asian schools. I've lived in Miami, Los Angeles, Abilene, Texas, and presently live in Houston. I've been an executive in some of the least diverse industries in the country—technology, commercial real estate, keynote professional speaking. I've worked both as an entrepreneur and as an executive in Fortune 50 companies. Throughout my career, I've helped hundreds of companies, schools, nonprofits, and governmental groups identify and overcome organizational practices that prevent them from fully accessing and maximizing the gifts of all their members. All that I have seen, done, and navigated has developed musculature for dealing with and reconciling difference—and it's quite literally my job.

And I felt confident in this work—until that moment. The revelation of the limitations of my own sense of justice sobered me. Despite all my personal and professional experience, the world was shouting out what I had been slowly becoming aware of: That the goal of inclusion itself, while noble, is inadequate. We need a bigger goal. We need to be Indivisible.

THE PROMISE REVISITED

America is not a naturally occurring phenomenon. It is a garden that must be tended, pruned, and nourished. Its genius lies in its ability to amend, but here, lately, we have felt stuck. Trapped by a division that pains us like shoes that are too small. What if there's another way?

"I pledge allegiance to the flag of the United States of America. And to the Republic, for which it stands, one nation, under God, indivisible, with liberty and justice for all."

Indivisible. What a beautiful word.

It is the most optimistic of words, capturing so much of what I want not just for my country but for my life. As a child shaped by divorce, I wanted a family that was Indivisible. At work, I want my team to be sharp, powerfully braided together, and Indivisible. And for my country? I truly desire liberty and justice for all. To me, it has become clear that if we could be Indivisible, we would be indestructible.

The word *Indivisible* isn't broadly used, and all the definitions I've seen have failed to capture its beautiful aspirational promise. We often struggle to find the right words, especially in the face of complex feelings. But in this book, I will try to show you what the word means to me.

To be Indivisible is to move through the world with a deep understanding of the value, strength, and beauty of others. It goes beyond knowledge. It is a practice of bridging difference to activate the unique capabilities of others and of yourself.

If we could be Indivisible, we would see our interconnectedness. We would move beyond apathy or even sympathy for each other. We would empathetically make choices knowing that we rise or fall together.

In 1985 a supergroup of music's biggest stars came together to record "We Are the World" as a fundraiser to address a devastating famine in Africa. A lyric from this song has stayed in my head since the '80s:

"There's a choice we're making. We're saving our own lives."

That is what it feels like to be Indivisible. It is understanding that when we honor the humanity of others, we really save ourselves.

•

What I want for myself, and for all of us, is to focus on what we are fighting for, not just what we are fighting against. Can we learn to turn to each other instead of turning on each other? We must reach for a higher goal, more worthy of our birthright. We must figure out a way to be different . . . together.

We should be Indivisible.

Like our physical bodies, interdependence is the genius of our design. The heart is no more important than the lungs. The muscles in our legs are the most powerful in our bodies and carry us through the world, but those legs are rendered useless without the aid of the tiny structures in our ears that keep us balanced. In the body, it's not about size or position. If you laid out your intestines, they would be over twenty feet long. That doesn't make them more important than the tiny pituitary gland, even though it weighs less than one gram. One does not matter more than the other. Each part of the body plays a vital role, and all are required for optimal performance.

And if a body works well through these constituent parts, it can climb Mount Everest, it can have a baby, it can go to the moon. The body can do absolutely incredible things. It's about the parts working together.

Can the body survive if a part is underperforming or missing? Sometimes yes. The body has an incredible ability to adapt. But it is unlikely that anyone would celebrate the loss of a hand or the frontal lobe of a brain. Even the removal of a superfluous appendix or wisdom teeth is a trauma to the body. The optimal condition is for all the parts to be thriving—Indivisible.

But being Indivisible is no easy feat.

We still haven't learned how connected we are—and it's thrown us into crisis, both individually and societally. We all have experienced incidents that separate us. That makes it hard to see, appreciate, and understand each other. Hurt and anger can be powerful barriers to connection. Our lack of commitment to each other has damaged every sphere of life, from education to economic opportunity to our health and well-being. It's clear that we're in a moment of challenge. People are powerfully polarized and civil discourse across difference is rare and precious. The stories we've long told ourselves about the American Dream seem to be just that—fictions that do not align with our real lives.

But here's the good news: I believe. I have worked with all kinds of people: liberals and conservatives, people of faith and atheists, old and young, from the North and South. And I believe.

I have seen people shift their mindsets and open up opportunities for others. I have seen people grow. It has fueled what some have called an inappropriate level of optimism, but I know that the only people who can change the world are the ones who think they can.

One tool I have used frequently is the Inclusion Continuum. I believe that inclusion can be placed on a continuum from 1–10, with 10 being the most evolved, and 1 being the folks who don't even know what the letters *DEI* together stand for. Most diversity, equity, and inclusion (DEI) efforts focus on people who are in the 6–10 end of the continuum, aka "preaching to the choir." This approach can feel good, but it leaves way too many people behind.

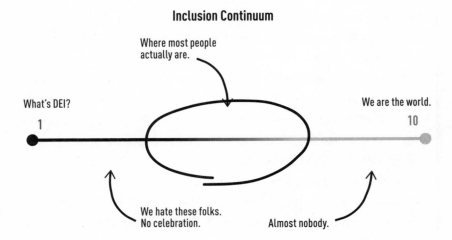

Inclusion Continuum

Where most people actually are.

What's DEI?

1

We are the world.

10

We hate these folks. No celebration.

Almost nobody.

We don't usually celebrate someone's move from a 1 to a 2 or a 2 to a 4, but without a mechanism to honor growth at all levels, there is little incentive for people in this range to move at all. I spend a lot of my time in the shallow end of that pool, and I have found it is bigger than we would like to believe. We have to create frameworks for everyone to grow, and we have to remove the shame of not knowing.

I share many stories of progress in this book, and I have changed the names and identifying details of people and companies with whom I have personally worked, because they have trusted me with their growth. I share their stories with you not to shame them or entertain you, but so you will share in that growth too.

Your journey through this book will require your openness, your patience, your understanding, and yes, your optimism. Let's be clear: The optimism I speak about is not some Pollyanna toxic positivity. The critical ingredient of optimism is action. While positivity stands around saying, "I hope I catch the bus," optimism starts running.

There are some who will scoff at this optimistic vision for the future. They will say that even as American schoolchildren recite that powerful pledge, we have been a nation that often rejects and abuses those who are different. It is an assertion I cannot disagree with.

While the ink was drying on the words "all men are created equal," women could not vote and more than 500,000 Africans were enslaved.[8] The words weren't true even as the Founding Fathers wrote them. But those of us who care have tried to make them more true with every generation.

Our ability to come through that darkness is proof that we have the capacity to go to an even brighter light.

Mistakes have been made—many of them. But the beauty of our story is that it isn't over. Together we choose its next iteration. We live in a metaphorical house that has great bones, so we all need to love it like an owner and make an investment in its future value.

It's clear to anyone paying attention that maintaining the status quo is not an option. We've inherited a set of ill-formed habits, practices,

xvi   What Does It Mean to Be Indivisible?

and mindsets that need to be examined, purged, and reimagined, so we can repair what's broken.

Indivisibility won't become our truth just because we say it is. It will only become true because we make it true. With our choices, our actions, our commitments. We must surrender the politics of cultural despair.

It is our work that makes our world.

Now, there may be those who are tempted to confuse being Indivisible with being homogeneous, making the incorrect assumption that the more alike we are, the stronger we will be. Let me correct that notion right now: Indivisible does not mean homogeneous. More accurately, it is the harmonized coordination of difference that creates a truly indestructible family, team, company, or country.

THE PROBLEM WITH TOLERANCE

> *"The function, the very serious function of racism is distraction. It keeps you from doing your work. It keeps you explaining, over and over again, your reason for being"*
>
> —TONI MORRISON

"William Tyson Croft. What name do you go by?"

"Everyone calls me Tyson."

It was my first day of college in Texas. As the teacher called the roll, I was confronted with the strangest phenomenon. The teacher would call the name and then ask what the student wanted to be called. Person after person, usually men, informed the teacher that they went by their middle name.

I was fascinated. I grew up in New York City and while we had nicknames, our teachers or professors wouldn't ask us what they were let alone use them. It got even more perplexing when my new classmates explained that even their parents called them by their middle names. If you want your child's name to be Kyle, why name him Thomas Kyle Jeffries? Why not just name him Kyle Thomas Jeffries? It was also strange how many of them went by two names à la Billy Ray Cyrus or

Tommy Lee Jones. I asked many questions, but I have to tell you that, more than thirty years later, I still don't understand. But I do understand that I don't have to understand.

If someone asks me to call them Tim or Bubba or Ricky Bobby, that's what I call them. I don't have to understand to offer respect.

One mistake we have made in our quest for tolerance is centering our understanding of someone else's experience as a precursor for offering them our respect.

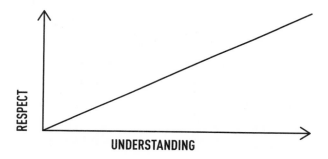

This is a costly mistake. All human beings are worthy of respect. Instead of thinking that the more you understand someone, the more worthy they are of respect, you should lead with respect. That is the only way to get to understanding.

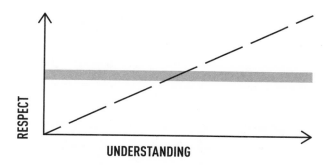

A homeless person is not deserving of more or less dignity because they are a veteran. They deserve dignity because they are a human being. When you think you have an understanding as to why someone has made certain choices or found themselves in a particular condition, it is easier to extend humanity to them. But think of the vanity of that. We all have a limited understanding of the world depending on our exposure to it.

As a woman of a certain age, I have not grown up with the lens of gender fluidity. Some of the concepts are entirely new to me. I am not natively familiar. Although I may struggle to understand some of the concepts, I never struggle with being respectful. My familiarity with a concept is not required to respect the humanity of another person.

My job is to actively be on my learning journey. To listen. To be curious. To courageously examine my beliefs to see where opportunities for growth lie. But irrespective of where I am on that journey, it's never appropriate to be disrespectful or unkind.

I don't need to understand the process of transitioning to understand trans people shouldn't be victims of violence. I don't have to understand the biology in order to use the pronouns they request of me. It costs me nothing to be kind.

I am always open to learning and you should be too. But there is a minimum way to move through the world as you learn. You need a plan for what you will do before you understand. My suggestion? Respect the humanity, autonomy, and right to self-determination of every human being.

When you come out of a past where disparate treatment was codified into law, it is a Herculean accomplishment to move beyond that damaged past and to encourage people to be tolerant of each other. Our growth in these spaces has been admirable but, nevertheless, insufficient. The very hard work that has been done by brave committed leaders throughout the years has finally gotten us to the place where we can conceive a broader, more ambitious vision.

We have outgrown the language of DEI. The very verbiage belies its finite utility. Diverse from whom? Equal to whom? Belonging where? It places one group at the center with all others working to gain access to that center and its spoils. These terms have been and continue to be critically important concepts, but they are tools, not targets. They are the road. Not the destination.

These tools—diversity, equity, inclusion, even patriotism—were always supposed to bring us to a higher version of ourselves. Much in the same way exercise, diet, and adequate hydration are tools but a healthy life is the goal. When you commit to the larger goal, it becomes easier, more logical to engage in the activities that get you there.

Our current approach to diversity and inclusion centers some groups over others. We have settled for the paltry goal of selectively allowing admission to increase the size of the center. If we are Indivisible, there is no center. The way we currently approach DEI celebrates and normalizes suboptimal performance. We can do better.

We have been complicit in as much as we have accepted the framing of there being some center that determines admission or rejection. We have accepted and/or perpetuated a broken frame—sometimes with malice, but more often with apathy and a poor grasp of the realities of our shared experience. We have learned to make a bad system work. Like the roots of a tree forced to push through concrete or wrap

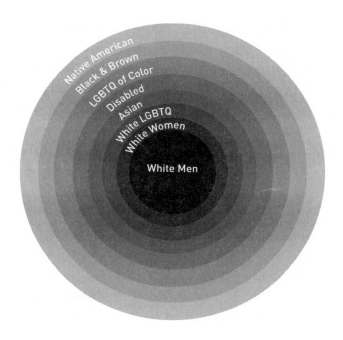

around pipes for survival, we are alive, but we have learned to normalize suboptimal living.

The current practice of positioning anyone as gatekeepers to the American Dream is coming head-to-head with the story of meritocracy that has been marketed as that dream throughout the world. The truth is meeting the myth in the public square, and the battle is raging. But the beauty of our system is its ability to evolve. The opportunity we have is to live up to the glory of our story.

We can choose a better way.

THE POWER WITHIN OUR REACH

This work is not easy. There are times when I feel fatigued, discouraged, or ill-equipped. It can be tempting to succumb to the twin demons of hopelessness and helplessness. When those moments hit me, I think about my personal hero, Harriet Tubman.

Harriet Tubman was an enslaved woman turned abolitionist who defied the odds and escaped slavery. Born in the 1800s on a plantation in Maryland, Harriet was brutally injured by an overseer as a child. He cracked her skull, resulting in a brain injury that caused her to have seizures and fainting spells for the rest of her life.

At the age of twenty-seven, Harriet ran to freedom, by herself, in a feat that should amaze us all. Harriet was illiterate. She had never been more than a mile from the plantation she was born on. She had no map, no horse, and knew no one in the North. She had no forged papers and had she been caught, she would have been brought back to the plantation, maimed, or possibly, killed.

But still, Harriet ran. That journey of ninety miles to Philadelphia should have felt impossible to someone in her situation, but still, she ran. And in a feat of extraordinary courage, she made her way to the North and earned her freedom.

The story could end there and be incredible. A petite, disabled woman ran to freedom alone and took back her life from those who had stolen it from her.

But the story doesn't end there. Harriet, unbelievably, went back. She actually went back to free others. She went on to be a conductor of the Underground Railroad which was a network of people, both Whites and free Blacks, who worked together to help runaways from slaveholding states travel to states in the North and to Canada to freedom. Because the Railroad was a secret enterprise, we do not have perfect records of all her trips, but it is widely believed that this young woman saved over seventy people in thirteen trips over ten years.[9] At first, she took the same route she had taken alone. She went back to the plantation of her birth to free her family and friends, bringing them to Philadelphia, but over time, as laws changed and pressure mounted, she was forced to transport these people the three hundred miles all the way to Canada.

Can you imagine? After finally finding freedom, risking it all, not once, but thirteen times. Each time angering the authorities more, her bravery threatening the entire system. On one trip taking eleven people, on another taking seven, all with a bounty on her head.

Everyone Else	Harriet Tubman
I can't read.	I'm RUNNING.
I can't write.	
I have a disability.	
I'm only 27 years old.	
I'll be all alone.	
I've never been more than a mile from the plantation.	
I don't have a map.	
I don't have any travel papers.	
They will maim or kill me if I'm caught.	
I don't have a cart or a horse.	
I don't know anyone on the journey.	
I don't know what I will be able to eat or drink.	
I'm afraid.	

If Harriet could take on this set of challenges to change her world, what can you and I do? Do we have less knowledge, fewer resources, or less access than this young illiterate woman did? Are we somehow less capable? I say no. All too often, we allow the too-loud voices of skeptics to persuade us of our powerlessness and our inability to create change. If we are going to be effective, there are critical lessons we must learn from Harriet's life:

Commitment: It must be done

To Harriet, slavery was unacceptable. The injustice could not stand. She had seen its horrors first hand and although she was free, she could not merely enjoy her safe, elevated position without a care for those suffering under inequality.

Do we feel the same? Do we feel like change MUST happen? Does your commitment to being Indivisible fall somewhere between picking up the dry cleaning and going to the gym, or is it a priority? A strongly held value you believe must be done? What do you need to see corrected in your lifetime?

Courage: It must be done by me

Being Indivisible is not a spectator sport. Harriet taught us that if change is to happen, we must be agents of that change. Unfortunately, many of us stand around waiting for someone else to come. Well, no one else is coming. While you're waiting on your Messiah, your Messiah is waiting on you.

Do we have the courage to personally do the hard things? Are we brave enough to risk actual consequences for our advocacy? Will we give up armchair advocacy to stand up for what's right and be bold enough to create the world we want to see?

Certainty: I have to believe it can happen

Harriet believed in the promise of freedom enough to risk her life for it over and over again. She believed the situation could be changed.

The only people who can change the world are the ones who think they can.

Are you one of those people? Do you believe that change is actually possible?

Creativity: I have to figure out how to do it

Harriet was a master of disguises. She used many throughout her journeys. Although she could not read or write, she was a cunning, creative woman. As the hunt for her became more intense, she was forced to develop more intricate plans to get enslaved people to freedom. She was a problem-solver who, I'm sure, could have instead leveraged those gifts for her personal gain.

Are we problem-solvers or excuse-makers? Do we leverage our gifts to find creative approaches to becoming stronger together?

Consistency: I will do it even when it gets hard

For Harriet to go back once was incredible, but thirteen times? We can learn so much from her consistency over time. Sometimes, we are held hostage by the size and expectations of our goals. We feel like if the results are not massive, or they do not happen overnight, then our efforts did not matter. I am in awe at the number of people she saved on each trip not because those numbers were so big, but because they were so small. I wonder if four or five people would have been enough for me. To some, taking all that risk for as few as three people would have hardly seemed worth it, but to the people who were saved from a life of torture, rape, and bondage? It meant everything.

Chances are, you will probably not get your seventy all at once. It is easy to have a burst of energy or a flash of activity, but to be truly Indivisible, we must consistently do the work over time, even when it gets hard, unpopular, or discouraging. Are you willing to be consistent? Are you willing to take small steps every day?

•

The first step in getting where you want to be is deciding not to stay where you are. The suggestions I share in this book will not be finite nor will they be exhaustive. They are a prompt, a beginning of a new conversation. Please resist the temptation to see them as an end.

We have inherited a powerful, tragic, beautiful, flawed, magnificent story, and it is our generation's turn to write the next chapter. We have everything we need to write it.

Let's begin.

Part 1

CHOOSE UNCOMFORTABLE TRUTH OVER BELOVED LIES

Chapter 1

Let Go of Broken Stories

"All stories are true. Some actually happened."

—SHEILA S. OTTO

"**YOU NEED TO FIRE THAT CONSULTANT DENISE HAMILTON!**"
In my role as an inclusion strategist, I often encounter quite a bit of resistance to what I have to say. But this case hit a new level. I had been engaged by a corporation with 17,000 employees to produce a series of videos about allyship and inclusion. Prior to rolling out the training to the whole organization, the executive team was given the opportunity to review the videos. The purpose of the videos was to explore the veracity of the stories we've all been told over the years. My goal? To encourage us all to examine our stories, even the dearest ones, so we can better set a path forward. One that is based on truth.

One of the examples was the baffling story of George Washington and his teeth. Now if you are a person of a certain age, you know that an entire generation of schoolchildren was taught that George Washington's teeth were made of wood. This is entirely false. In fact, our first president's teeth were made primarily of two materials: ivory (rhinoceros and elephant tusks) and human teeth, including those pulled from living enslaved people without anesthesia.[10]

At Mount Vernon, Washington's plantation, records reveal ledger entries for payment for the purchase of some of the teeth, but it is more likely that the owners of the enslaved were paid than the enslaved themselves. Washington was not notably generous. Despite the harsh weather conditions of Virginia and the grueling toll of plantation work, records also indicate Washington provided only one suit of clothing and one pair of shoes to "his property" per year.[11] It is highly unlikely that he paid people he owned entirely and over whom he had the complete physical threat of coercion.

Learning that George Washington's false teeth were not wood, that some of the teeth were actually pulled from the mouths of human beings is shocking. Why was this story even told? Especially when you consider that it was an unnecessary lie. Who was asking this question? Who needed this story? Why were entire generations of children told this false narrative well into the twentieth century?

I share it in hopes that the audience will allow themselves to examine their stories—all of them. The simple message: Don't believe everything you think.

You have received millions of messages throughout the course of your life. Part of your personal evolution is to have the courage to discern truth from fiction and to conduct your decision-making based on the truth as much as possible. This is no easy task. Not only have you received your personal set of messages, but so has the person next to you and the person across town, and the person on the other side of the globe. The work before us, as we attempt to bridge difference and exist together, is to reconcile the truth of our stories.

That reconciliation can be difficult, as we see in this case. One of the executives who screened the video was furious. He reached out to my liaison at the company to demand that my contract be terminated immediately. He called me a liar, spreading propaganda to advance a political position to tarnish America. Nothing could be further from the truth. I don't believe the story of America to be so fragile that it cannot withstand correction.

I live in Texas, so this was definitely not my first rodeo. Upon the creation of the videos, I provided all citations to back up any assertions that had been presented. My contact shared those resources with the executive.

What happened next was fascinating.

He called back the next day and said he had reviewed the material and agreed that I was factually accurate. He still felt, however, that the videos should not be shared with the organization. His reasoning? "The information is a tangent. It is not helpful and does not advance the conversation." I was struck by this. One day, the information is so inflammatory that I need to be fired. The very next day, it's irrelevant and not worth sharing with the team.

Who we are is shaped by the stories we hold dear. To me, it seemed obvious that he wanted to protect this narrative. He is not alone. We all do this. Our identities are often wrapped up in our mythologies. The executive was acting as the keeper of the story, and this truth was a threat.

To him, I was a thief. I had stolen his story. It didn't matter if it was true or not. What mattered was, it was his and I was taking it.

These sorts of conflicts are happening all around us. We are fighting over history books and statues, policies and boundaries. Reconciling truths is challenging business. Civil discourse has never been less civil. We are struggling foundationally with what is true about the story of America. About our systems, our faith, our legacy, and our promise.

I believe we can come together, but first, we must examine the stories through which we see ourselves and be open to the possibility that they may not be true. When we discover inconsistencies, we must find the courage to let go of our broken stories. We must crave and embrace truth, even when that truth is uncomfortable. Even when it hurts.

Truth is a critical ingredient to being Indivisible.

WE ARE THE SUM OF OUR STORIES

Our stories tell us who we are. Who gets to be the hero and what a captain looks like. They teach us who is good and who is bad, and who deserves to live happily ever after. They help us make sense of our world. The problem with that is, our stories are broken.

Stories transmit culture and values. This becomes difficult because as our understanding of our world grows, our stories stay the same, holding us in a world we need to move forward from.

I think about my cohort of executives. We are all in our fifties and sixties—just think, the average age of a US senator is sixty-five[12]—and these are the stories that shaped us:

- The toy gun was the number one toy in America (1950s and 1960s).[13]
- Black people were represented on television primarily as thugs and criminals (1960s to 1990s).[14]
- Martin Luther King Jr. was among the most hated public figures in America and was assassinated at the age of thirty-nine (1968).[15]
- Women couldn't have a checking account in their name or buy a house on their own until 1974.[16]
- Tiger Woods was not allowed to use the clubhouses of many of the country clubs where golf tournaments were played because of his Black heritage. (1980s).[17]
- Vanessa Williams became the first non-White Miss America (1983).[18]
- Rodney King was savagely beaten by police officers, and even though there was video footage, the officers were acquitted (1991).[19]
- Spousal abuse wasn't recognized as a crime until 1994.[20]
- Bill Clinton's sex scandal ushered in an era of online shaming (1998).[21]

Information about Native American people was gleaned from watching *The Lone Ranger* and countless Westerns that depicted them as "savages," with the settlers presented as heroes, not invaders. Americans learned about Africa from Tarzan and his ludicrous designation as King of the Jungle as he spoke to animals and battled the "stupid" natives. Millions gathered weekly to watch *The Dukes of Hazzard* as they normalized the Confederate flag painted across the roof of their car, the General Lee. The stories we were given shaped our world, and our stories do not give us up easily.

I attended a predominantly White university, and if you go to any such school in America, you will see the Black kids sitting in the cafeteria, huddled together for warmth. White students often asked, "Why do all the Black kids sit together?" I thought it was a funny question because the White kids didn't realize they were all sitting together too. Aligning with people who are like you is easy. You have a shorthand. A common language. You don't have to explain yourself.

If I say "Tory Burch flats" to a group of professional women, most will know what I mean. If I say "2K" to a group of gamers, they instantly know what I mean. The rest of us might be lost, but in-groups understand each other.

It's like the old TV show *Name That Tune*. The more familiar you are with the genre, the easier it is for you to name the song in just a few notes. We are attracted to people who share our shorthand. We really like people who "get" us.

The problem with this is we can get sucked into the siren song of sameness. Deferring to people who are like us, falling in line instead of leading. It is this very comfort and familiarity that can sometimes keep us from being Indivisible.

Indivisible leaders challenge their stories and look for places and spaces where their stories no longer serve them.

In my office, I have a shrine of three things to remind me to challenge my assumptions.

1. Airbnb Sticker

The first item is an Airbnb sticker. I can picture myself as a Venture capitalist or Angel Investor being pitched the idea of the startup by the founders. I have to be honest. If someone had said Sally and Simon Stranger from the internet are going to pay to stay in your house when you're not there, or even WORSE, when you are there, it would have been a hard no for me. I would have loudly said no way! And I would have been wrong. Loud and terribly wrong. $6 billion a year wrong.

Lesson #1. I don't know everything.

2. Vicks VapoRub

I remember the times I got sick as a child. I knew things were real when my mother or grandmother would break out the Vicks VapoRub. Their warm hands would rub it all over my back and chest and just knew all would soon be well with the world. I would inhale the medicine from this thick calming balm and I would instantly be healed.

But it turns out we were wrong. Numerous studies have been performed on Vicks VapoRub and it has been found to have no medicinal value.[22] The calming smell and the comforting touch during its application are soothing, but not healing.

Lesson #2. What I know for sure may not be true.

3. Barack Obama Bobble Head Doll

I remember where I was when Barack Obama announced his run for President, but more importantly, I remember what I did. I laughed. Out loud. I thought the whole thing was ridiculous. I was sure there would never be a Black President in my lifetime.

And I was wrong. He was elected, not just once, but twice. The world had expanded beyond my ability to imagine it.

Lesson #3. The disappointments of yesterday are not predictors of tomorrow. We always have the power to create a new story.

OUR STORIES ARE BROKEN

One treasure trove of reality-defining stories is fairy tales. One that bothers me, in particular, is the story of Rapunzel. You remember *Rapunzel*. She was the one with the inappropriately long hair. Rapunzel was trapped in a tower with no doors. The only way in or out was by climbing up Rapunzel's hair. She used her hair to help her mother the witch get in and out of the tower. Later she used her hair to help a handsome prince get in and out of the tower.

I was in my forties before I ever asked the key question:

Why didn't she use her hair to get herself out of the tower?

It was her hair right? Why didn't she free herself? I didn't challenge the story at all growing up. Like so many other people, I just internalized the lesson shared by so many stories. Like *Cinderella*, *Snow White*, and *Sleeping Beauty*, you have to wait for someone else to save you. You can help everyone else but not yourself.

Another one of my favorites is *The Little Mermaid*. Ariel trades her voice (and her mermaid status) to the Sea Witch for just a chance to marry Prince Eric. At the time of her sacrifice, she had never even spoken to the Prince. Luckily, in the end it all works out. She is able to earn true love's kiss and gets to live as a human, happily ever after with Eric.

What's the moral of this story? You can have the man of your dreams. All you have to do is give up your voice. Are you starting to get nauseous yet?

My personal favorite? *Beauty and the Beast.*

Belle finds her father in the dungeon of the palace. He is sick, cold, and starving. He is dying. Belle begs the Beast for her father's release. The Beast refuses and forces Belle to trade her freedom for her father's, throwing him out of the castle without letting Belle even say goodbye. Now she is a prisoner in the castle. The Beast is an angry, aggressive character. One night the Beast scares her so badly that she runs into the frozen wolf-infested woods in the middle of the night to get away from him.

Now walk me through how they end up in love and living happily ever after? It sounds like Stockholm Syndrome to me.

The moral of this story: True love will turn a Beast into a prince.

I don't know about you, but I do not want my daughter to be in the business of turning Beasts into princes. Yet my daughter (and most of yours) has probably watched these movies and others like it hundreds of times growing up. We don't even realize the stories and the fairy tales that shape our reality. We don't even think about it. All they have to do is set it to music and they've got us. But these messages, they matter. Our mythology matters, and it shapes us. Even as we make progress, it's hard to retire *Rapunzel*. The old stories do not release us easily.

But the stories that impact us don't just live in books.

It was the year 2019. "Operation Varsity Blues" hit the headlines as more than fifty people were indicted.[23] The college cheating scam involved wealthy families paying to get their children into elite colleges and universities. The elaborate scheme involved bribery, money laundering, and document fabrication.

Essentially, these rich parents would pay university coaches and administrators to designate their children as desirable athletic recruits. Some families even went as far as to stage photographs of their children playing the sport to submit with their application. Other students were paid to take standardized tests for them. Any and all measures were taken for their children to gain acceptance to the country's most elite schools.

It was gross. These wealthy children have been raised with every advantage. They attended expensive private schools, lived in wealthy, safe neighborhoods. They had access to the best tutors and extracurricular activities money could buy. They had good nutrition and top-notch medical care. They could easily afford to foot the bill to attend any school that accepted them. Their parents are celebrities, successful business owners, and executives all with the connections to secure internships and ultimately jobs (for those that wanted them).

It's amazing how people with so much advantage could be so committed to compounding that advantage even further. They had everything. But they still chose to cheat.

They felt compelled to because it was their turn to perpetuate the story we tell ourselves about elite schools in America.

If you go to the Ivy League, you're more valuable.

You're better.

Everyone there is so much better.

But if 30-40 percent of the kids are legacy or athletic admission, how different are they really from the rest of us?[24] Are they only there because their mom or dad went there? Or because they're rich? Does a degree from these schools really ensure that these are the best and brightest our country has to offer?

These schools are private and they can conduct their business how they choose to, but what the college cheating scandal revealed to all of us is that we have been given a broken story.

We've been told that a C student who got into Yale because his father donated money for a building is more valuable than a young woman who grew up in poverty, stepped over drugs, dodged the gangs, and still graduated top of her class.

Maybe she went to the University of Houston or Iowa State. She doesn't have any sexy internships, because her parents couldn't call a buddy at Google to help her get one. She doesn't play lacrosse or row crew or have any other fancy extracurricular activities because she worked two jobs to take care of her siblings and pay her own way. Despite all these challenges, she still excels. Nevertheless, his pedigree of attending an "Ivy League" school trumps all of that.

That's the story I hear repeated throughout many of the organizations I work with. Some employers won't even interview people who don't come from certain schools. Many schools never receive announcements for job openings or internships. This is a mistake.

And now we have proof. Only eleven of the CEOs of Fortune 500 companies attended an Ivy League school.[25] The school that has produced the most is actually the University of Wisconsin. Other top contributors to the ranks of success are the University of Miami and the University of North Carolina, the State University of New York (SUNY) system, and many, many others. There is excellence everywhere from coast to coast.

Over 70 percent of Black physicians and dentists earn their degrees from Historically Black Colleges and Universities (HBCUs).[26] And Black doctors matter. Black babies die at three times the rate of White newborns. That number is decreased by 58 percent when the doctor is Black.[27]

Excellence is all around us, but we must be willing to surrender our broken stories to access the fullness of possibility.

OUR STORIES ARE INCOMPLETE

Terry sat in the session toward the back of the room. She was lovely, conscientious, and smart. And she was a Jehovah's Witness.

The class conversation shifted to the Holocaust, and a gentleman in the class said he still couldn't believe that so much hate could be directed at one group of people. Terry stiffened.

The teacher noticed and asked, "Terry, is there something you'd like to add to the conversation?"

She stared back at the teacher. After a pregnant silence, she tentatively answered. "Nobody ever talks about the Jehovah's Witnesses that were sent to the concentration camps." She fidgeted nervously. "Our religion was targeted as well, but nobody ever seems to talk about that.

Her words hung in the air. She was right. One of every two Jehovah's Witnesses in Germany was sent to the concentration camps.[28] And they are largely left out of the story.

It's easy to see why she feels that nobody knows and nobody cares. The story of 6 million Jews being killed by Hitler and the Nazis has been branded on the minds of every American school child. But do you know the number of those murdered is actually almost double that? Approximately 11.5 million people from targeted groups died in the camps. People with disabilities, homosexuals, Romani (formerly referred to as Gypsies), Freemasons, almost all the Black Germans, and, yes, Jehovah's Witnesses.

It's not hard to sympathize with Terry's feelings. We say "never forget" to people who have been forgotten. Erasure hurts.

But how had the story been so profoundly redacted? I called a dear friend of mine who is Jewish to learn more about this issue. I started the conversation by asking her how many people died in the concentration camps, and she quickly answered 6 million. I said no, the number is actually 11.5 million.

She didn't believe me. She asked me to send her my sources for that number. After reading what I sent, she called me back in disbelief. She had no idea.

Later that evening she attended a Shabbat dinner with her family. She also posed my question to them. Out of the eleven Jewish people in attendance, only one other person knew the number was 11.5 million.

My friend was shaken by this information. The Holocaust was such a defining experience for the Jewish people, it was jarring to be so wrong about such a salient detail. And to be so innocently wrong. There was no malice here. No ill intent. The story had been summarized to highlight those with the most profound loss.

Consider the reasoning behind police interviewing the same witness multiple times. They do so because witnesses frequently leave out key details. Not because they are trying to be dishonest or sabotage the case, but because they underestimate the significance of that detail to the case. People tell stories from their own vantage points, using their own judgment to determine what's significant.

But that is the complex nature of stories. There are hundreds of characteristics that define me. I am a professional speaker. I have a master's degree. I love pizza. I wear makeup. I've been featured in *Harvard Business Review*. I have a daughter who defeated a catastrophic illness. I drink way too much Coca-Cola. All of these things are true about me, but only a few of them make it into my bio.

It is human nature to tell an incomplete story. The reality is:

- **People tell their own stories.** It is a normal behavior to tell a story through the lens that you experienced it, which is your own.
- **Small stories are often lost in big ones.** Human beings are not famous for nuance. We live and operate in broad strokes. Amplifying smaller stories is always a challenge.
- **It's easier to simplify.** Simplicity is infectious. This is why memes go viral. This is why we have books full of quotes from famous people. We love a simple, tight message, which means we always leave things out.

What does that mean for those of us who are committed to being Indivisible? It means we need to be intentional about seeking out the smaller story. We have to create opportunities to be exposed to the unique experiences of different groups. Especially if those groups are small in size or power. We also need to be deliberate in sharing positive stories whenever possible.

I do not believe there is always blame to be placed for the incomplete nature of a story. But unfortunately, there are times when stories are redacted to intentionally create harm. The ultimate example of a maliciously incomplete story is the Slave Bible.

In the 1800s, slave owners feared that Bible verses about freedom would incite the enslaved Africans to rebel.[29] On the other hand, certain passages of Scripture encouraged submission to authority, such as Ephesians 6:5: "Servants, be obedient to them that are your masters according to the flesh, with fear and trembling, in singleness of your heart, as unto Christ."

Rather than withholding the entire Bible, some plantation owners allowed the enslaved to have the Slave Bible, which was compiled from selected parts of God's word to inspire submission. The scale and breadth of this redaction were incredible. According to the Smithsonian, about 90 percent of the Old Testament is missing and 50 percent of the New Testament is missing. In other words, there are 1,189 chapters in a standard protestant Bible, but the Slave Bible only contains 232.[30]

The Slave Bible was commissioned on behalf of the Society for the Conversion of Negro Slaves for use by missionaries who wanted to teach enslaved Africans to read, with the ultimate goal of introducing them to Christianity.

Some examples of verses that were eliminated:
- "For freedom Christ has set us free; stand firm therefore, and do not submit again to a yoke of slavery." Galatians 5:1
- "There is neither Jew nor Greek, there is neither bond nor free, there is neither male nor female: for ye are all one in Christ Jesus." Galatians 3:28
- "Woe unto him that buildeth his house by unrighteousness, and his chambers by wrong; that useth his neighbor's service without wages and giveth him not for his work." Jeremiah 22:13
- "And he that stealeth a man, and selleth him, or if he be found in his hand, he shall surely be put to death" Exodus 21:16

In this instance, bad actors leveraged the belief that the Bible is the inspired word of God to advance their own personal financial agenda. It isn't only the stories we tell that harm us, but also the stories we leave out. The power to omit is a tempting power indeed.

Virginia Woolf once said, "I would venture to guess that Anonymous, who wrote so many poems without signing them, was often a woman." It's shocking to imagine now, but there was a time when women were prohibited from being published, often resorting to the use of pen names. I think it is safe to assume that there were smart, thoughtful, profound women in the time of Plato, Mark Twain, and Einstein, but the practice was not to capture the thoughts of women and if you did, they were often misattributed to a man.

Countless inventions, recipes, music, and processes have been poached from their creators. From Elvis to Aunt Jemima to *The Matrix*. The list goes on. Even Jack Daniel's, America's whiskey, gets the credit and wealth from a product created by a Black man named Nearest Green. As we learn more about these incredible creators, it is important to make room for them, to honor them.

In his docuseries *Exterminate All the Brutes*, acclaimed filmmaker Raoul Peck said "Every history is a particular bundle of silences." History is written by the winners.

Omission is a powerful tool for sanitizing realities. Some of our precious stories are lost forever. We may never know the whole truth. That is why humility in the face of new information is so important and critical to being truly Indivisible. We must value each other enough to allow for the fullness of all stories to be told even when it is unpleasant and invalidates a beloved story of our own.

OUR STORIES ARE OUTRIGHT LIES

> "Hello, I'm Tim Bozik and I lead Global Product Development
> at Pearson and I want to apologize. In an attempt to help the
> nursing students think through the many facets of caring for
> the patients, we've reinforced a number of stereotypes about
> ethnic and religious groups. It was wrong."
>
> —TIM BOZIK, 2017

Tim was right. It was wrong. A widely used Pearson nursing textbook, published in 2014, had perpetuated some of the worst medical myths. In a chart about pain, sweeping generalizations were shared: "Hispanics may believe that pain is a form of punishment and that suffering must be endured if they are to enter heaven." "Jews may be vocal and demanding of assistance." "Blacks often report higher pain intensity than other cultures."[31] In his apology, Bozik continued, "We apologize for the offense this has caused and we have removed the material in question from current versions of the book, electronic versions of the book and future editions of this. . . . In addition, we now are actively reviewing all of our nursing curriculum products to identify and remove any remaining instances of this inappropriate content that might appear in other titles."

But the assertions got even more ridiculous. "Native Americans may prefer to receive medications that have been blessed by a tribal shaman." "Indians who follow Hindu practices believe that pain must be endured in preparation for a better life in the next cycle." "Chinese patients may not ask for medicine because they do not want to take the nurse away from a more important task."

Think of the damage these harmful tropes could create. Based on this information, a nurse could dismiss the pleas of a Jewish person because they are being "dramatic" or ignore the complaints of pain from a Black person as drug-seeking. Imagine the potential negative outcomes. It is interesting to notice that every other racial and ethnic group is discussed, except for White people. The assumption is that White people's experience of pain is the standard that every other group's behavior is compared to.

This was printed in a textbook, but that doesn't mean it's true. Unfortunately, textbooks are often an efficient vehicle for lies.

- "But the 'peculiar institution,' as Southerners came to call it, like all human institutions should not be oversimplified. While there were cruel masters who maimed or even killed their slaves (although killing and maiming were against the law in every state), there were also kind and generous owners." (Prentice Hall Classics: *A History of the United States*, 2007)
- "Though most slaves were whipped at some point in their lives, a few never felt the lash. Nor did all slaves work in the fields. Some were house servants or skilled artisans. Many may not have even been terribly unhappy with their lot, for they knew no other." (*World Geography*, 2016)
- "The Atlantic Slave Trade between 1500s and 1800s brought millions of workers from Africa to the southern United States to work on agricultural plantations." (*World Geography*, 2016)
- "They had worked hard in Africa, and so the work on the Virginia plantations did not hurt them. The Negroes learned also to enjoy the work and play of the plantations . . . Virginia offered a better life for the Negroes than did Africa . . . " (*Virginia: History, Government, Geography*, published in 1956 and used in classrooms through the late 1970s)
- "A feeling of strong affection existed between masters and slaves in a majority of Virginia homes . . . The regard that master and slaves had for each other made plantation life happy and prosperous." (*Virginia: History, Government, Geography*, published in 1956 and used in classrooms through the late 1970s)
- " . . . his condition had advantages . . . he enjoyed long holidays . . . he did not work so hard as the average free laborer, since he did not have to worry about losing his job. In fact, the slave enjoyed what we might call comprehensive social security. Gen-

erally speaking, his food was plentiful, his clothing adequate, his cabin warm, his health protected and his leisure carefree." (*Cavalier Commonwealth: History and Government of Virginia*, 1957)

You may think some of these books are old, but there are twenty-one senators between seventy and eighty and four over the age of eighty. In fact, 50 percent of the Senate is sixty-five years or older. These are the stories that shaped them. They were raised reading these textbooks.

I wish I could say that these compromised textbooks were a thing of the distant past. In textbooks published as recently as 2015, slaves were referred to as "workers and immigrants" who experienced "involuntary relocation." A Texas McGraw-Hill textbook stated that slaves just "helped work the field and do chores."[32] In 2021, Texas and Oklahoma passed laws restricting the teaching of certain portions of our history in schools, and similar bills have been introduced in other states, including Florida, Arizona, and Tennessee.[33] Some go as far as to criminalize the teaching of any content that makes people feel "discomfort" or "guilt" based on their race, sex, or national origin. This is particularly challenging because the truth is not always comfortable.

We are deep in the work of finding our accurate stories.

THE TRUTH ABOUT LIES

If you ask the average person, they will tell you that honesty, integrity, and truthfulness are incredibly important to them. But unfortunately, the sheer volume of misinformation that circulates freely indicates that that isn't necessarily true. There are reasons that lies proliferate.

They're delicious: We often prefer a beloved lie to a distasteful truth. Ideas that confirm our existing beliefs or are given to us by people we trust are always going to be attractive. And if they're salacious, even more so. We love a juicy morsel about an enemy or a glowing factoid about a friend.

They're enduring: We are still stamping out untruths from decades ago. George Washington did not cut down the cherry tree. Nero didn't fiddle while Rome burned. Marie Antoinette never said, "Let them eat cake." If you put a frog in water and start raising the temperature, the frog will jump out. We have so many stories that we circulate as fact. No matter how many times they are debunked, these stories live in our consciousness.

They move faster than the truth: Mark Twain famously said, "A lie can travel halfway around the world before the truth puts on its shoes." Twain grossly underestimated the changes that technology would bring. The internet allows for disinformation to travel around the world six times faster than the truth. Tweets containing falsehoods are 70 percent more likely to be retweeted than truthful tweets.

They multiply: We have come to a point in history where people literally use lies and misinformation as proof of other belief systems. Lawmakers develop policy based on fraudulent stories. For example, a rumor that started online made its way to a legislative hearing in Tennessee where two state lawmakers discussed the "growing crisis" of public schools providing litter boxes for children who identify as cats, claiming it was happening across the state. None of it was true, but lies beget lies.[34]

Truth takes work. Our stories matter. In her TED talk, Chimamanda Ngozi Adichie warns us about the danger of a single story, "The single story creates stereotypes, and the problem with stereotypes is not that they aren't true, but they are incomplete. They make one story become the only story."

We have many stories. We cannot be afraid of them being told. Indivisible leaders seek to embrace them all.

ASK YOURSELF

- What are some stories that you grew up with as a child that you look back on now with discomfort? What stories have been the most difficult for you to release?
- How have you handled it when you accept a new truth, but the people you care about haven't accepted that truth yet?
- Have you ever mourned the loss of a beloved story? What was your process?
- Are you glad to receive correction when your understanding of a story is incorrect or do you resist or resent it?

Chapter 2

Surrender Strange Artifacts

"A nation reveals itself not only by the men it
produces, but also by the men it honors."

—JOHN F. KENNEDY

W E WOULD LEARN A LOT FROM OUR MISTAKES IF WE WOULD STOP excusing them. One of the less admirable qualities of American culture is our odd tendency to enshrine our failures. Whether it's confederate statues or Black people using the N-word, we have a strange relationship with the damaging parts of our culture. There are so many examples.

A friend shared an article with me. It was a "feel-good story" about a severely disabled girl in the third grade who needed a motorized wheelchair. As is the case for so many in the United States, her parents had terrible insurance and their request for coverage was denied. This unfortunate situation came to the attention of the robotics club at the local high school. They worked countless hours after school and on weekends to build her a custom motorized wheelchair.[35] Delightful story, right?

Wrong. Our older children should not have the responsibility to help our younger children navigate catastrophic health conditions. These teenagers should not be in charge of a sick child's mobility.

The fact that this story, this artifact, is presented as "good news" is emblematic of how we have normalized deep failures within our system. Yes, the high school kids were wonderful. Yes, it's lovely that the young girl received the wheelchair. It's horrific, however, that the system fails so profoundly, so consistently.

Even more tragic? We have become numb to it. We have learned to celebrate thriving in spite of the failing conditions around us instead of the actual remediation of the conditions. Celebrating the adaptations to our toxicity has taken the place of fixing our toxicity. How do we resist the temptation of the "feel-good story", to make the changes that will actually feel good?

MAY THE ODDS BE EVER IN YOUR FAVOR

The children and their parents huddled together in the loud, crowded auditorium. In their hands, they clutched the numbers they had been assigned. Some families were dressed up like they were going to church. Others laughed and played on their phones. Some children sat alone. Likely, latchkey kids whose parents could not afford to miss work even for an occasion as special as this.

The day had finally come.

"Number 231," the announcer said.

A happy family leapt to their feet and cheered.

"Number 73."

"Number 105."

Family after family pushed through the crowd to pick up their admission packet. They did it. They had gotten in.

As the announcer got closer to the end of the list, the room became stiff and tense. The remaining crowd grew quieter. You could feel dread replacing the hope and excitement that filled the room just an hour ago. Some were praying, rosaries wrapped around their hands. Praying their child's name would be called next. You could see tears filling the eyes of the anxious mothers as they started to fear the worst.

They had filled out all the applications, done all the paperwork, attended all the meetings. They couldn't get this close and not get in.

"Number 496. Number 19. That concludes our school lottery for this school year. Thank you for applying."

The room was broken. Fathers angrily shouted at the stage, while mothers quietly wept. Some people rushed the stage to double-check if they had been called. But they hadn't. Their child had not gotten in.

There was only one good school in the neighborhood. This was it. But they only had seventy-five spots for the 1100 applicants.

I stood in the back of the room in tears. A friend had invited me to watch the *Hunger Games*-esque process of getting an acceptable education in America's inner city, and I was ashamed. Ashamed that we relied on a rabbit's foot and a Ouija board to decide who gets to learn.

I did not know who had been in that room. Was it our generation's Einstein or Curie? Was the cure to cancer in this room? The answer to global warming? Are we so satisfied with the state of our world that we can afford to waste its most precious resource?

As the room emptied, a young girl sat toward the back of the room by herself. Her little hands held her number. I asked her if she was OK but I knew she wasn't. And I was worried that maybe she wouldn't be. . . .

This artifact was the strangest of them all. Rather than fix a broken system that has been ravaged because of its roots in racism and classism, we have erected these bingo halls of educational opportunity to make ourselves feel better. That night, seventy-five children and their families would celebrate, and we will lie to ourselves and say that this is enough. But it will not be true.

SUFFERING AS ENTERTAINMENT

We are experts at normalizing failure. Another place where we experience a strange phenomenon is with TV shows like *Dr. Pimple Popper*. If you've never seen the show, the concept is very simple: A highly skilled dermatologist takes extreme cases of severe conditions or deformities people have lived with for years and treats them at no charge. The show is a parade of huge cysts, growths, calluses, and even horns—the more gross and horrific, the more likely to get on the show. I must admit, seeing these life-altering conditions people have suffered for years neatly resolved in a thirty-minute episode is oddly satisfying.

But why have these people gone untreated for years? How could someone suffering as obviously as the patients featured on the show not seek medical attention? The answer: They are poor. The vast majority do not have health insurance and the ones that do quickly learn that their deforming conditions are excluded as "cosmetic" procedures. In other cases, the copays place treatment outside affordability.

So they suffer.

And we watch.

We watch but, oddly, we are not embarrassed. We celebrate the kindness of the doctor, the long-suffering of the patient, and the triumphant resolution of the case. We are ghoulishly entertained by the medical procedures, the grosser the better. We are happy for the new lease on life the patients have now that the life-limiting condition has been addressed.

But we are not embarrassed.

We say things like:

"How could they (the patient) let this go on for so long?"

"How could they work or find a mate with that horrible condition?"

"I would kill myself if I looked like that."

We do not look at these shows as an indictment of our systems. We don't wonder about the thousands of people crossing their fingers as they send in their request for treatment. We don't think about how many staff members and producers are hired to sift through those requests to decide who gets the golden ticket of healing. We're even less curious about what the criteria are. How does one decide who gets to be healed?

Reality TV has offered up a smorgasbord of suffering for our entertainment. Whether it is finding out "you are not the father," or laughing as women climb across tables to fight each other, the cultural practice of peering into dysfunction with delight is an odd one.

I wonder if, 100 years from now, people will look back in judgment of us the way we look back in judgment of the gladiator tournaments or Christians being fed to the lions in Roman times.

Are we not entertained?

MINE, MINE, MINE

So far, we've been talking about the metaphorical artifacts of American culture. Now let's turn our attention to the world and the countless physical artifacts filling the museums across the globe with the spoils of other cultures. The practice of housing mostly ill-gotten gain plundered from other cultures without shame is an artifact in its own right. Charging visitors admission to see the collection of the stuff you stole is strange indeed.

I have watched with some interest as the art community has wrestled with the rising call for stolen antiquities to be returned. As we learn more about the brutal history of how many of these items have been acquired, the question is: What do we do now?

There have been many interesting arguments made against the repatriation of these items:

- Many source communities that demand the return of their artifacts may not have the resources or expertise to preserve and protect these items properly.
- The possibility of looting and theft during the repatriation process. This concern arises because the repatriation of cultural objects can be a complex process involving multiple parties, including governments, museums, and private collectors. There have been instances in the past where repatriation efforts have been derailed due to theft or looting of the objects in question.
- Many source communities may not be adequately equipped to preserve and maintain these items.
- In an article by CNN, lawyer and human rights advocate Geoffrey Robertson argues that "Preservation of priceless antiquities is essential, and it would not be right to return them to coun-

tries plagued by civil war or to museums where they might not be properly cared for."[36]

- Furthermore, as the *New York Times* reports, some art dealers and curators have expressed concerns that returning artifacts could "eventually empty museums and galleries" as well as "fuel a global market in looted antiquities."[37]

- There are concerns that repatriation requests may be politically motivated, and that some countries may use the repatriation process to assert claims over artifacts that do not have clear ownership histories.

According to the British Museum, their collection totals at least eight million objects. Roughly 80,000 objects are on public display at the British Museum in Bloomsbury at any one time. This is 1 percent of the collection. In essence, they would rather keep these items in boxes in storage than give them back.

Some of the arguments have been interesting, but one in particular caught my eye. "We can't give the art back. These items are priceless and they don't know how to store and care for them properly." Imagine the arrogance. The very suggestion is that you do not have to give someone their own rightful possession because you are not convinced of their ability to take care of it. It's laughable and, unsurprisingly, paternalistic.

When I'm trying to understand a complex issue, one of my favorite techniques is "swap the nouns." I simply replace the subjects of the conversation with other parallel concepts so I can see if I feel the same about the issue. Let's try that in this situation.

You have a valuable cashmere sweater. I decide that I like it, so I take it from your house without your permission. You realize that I took it and ask for it back. I say, "A cashmere sweater is best stored in a cedar chest or closet. You have neither, so it should stay with me. I've been caring for it for two years. You don't have the necessary experience. I know how to care for it better than you." Then I refuse to return it.

Sounds ridiculous right? Imagine thinking you can keep something you stole because you think you would be a better steward of it.

In the case of these artifacts, you might say these are precious antiquities that would be lost to the world if they were damaged or destroyed. To that I say, they still don't belong to you. If you want to dip that sweater in mayonnaise in the backyard and set it on fire, you could. It's yours. If India wants to use the Noor diamond as a doorstop, they can. It's theirs.

During the January 6th insurrection, numerous precious artifacts and pieces of art were damaged or destroyed by the rioters who breached the Capitol. Could Canada march up to the building and start boxing up the remaining artifacts to keep them safe?

In 2019, Notre Dame Cathedral burned down with countless priceless, irreplaceable artifacts that were stored there. Does that mean that Jamaica can roll up to the Louvre and start packing up the *Mona Lisa*?

In the figure below, I have diagramed the different ways I've heard people address this issue.

One group says, "We took it. We won. It's ours."

Another group says, "We took it. We won. We're sorry."

The third group says, "We took it. We shouldn't have. We're sorry."

And the last group says, "We took it. We shouldn't have. We will give it back."

Where you plot your position is significant when you think about being Indivisible. How much do you respect other people and their autonomy in making decisions for themselves and their lives? Do you respect the boundaries of others? How often do you put yourself in the position to parent other adult people? What do you think is our responsibility to correct past wrongs?

We took it.	We took it.	We took it.	We took it.
We won.	We won.	We shouldn't have.	We shouldn't have.
It's ours.	We're sorry.	We're sorry.	We will give it back.

← ——————————————————————————→

In 2022, the Vanderkindere Auction House in Brussels was forced to cancel the sale of skulls of Africans killed during the colonial period in what is now the Democratic Republic of Congo.[38] The Belgian history of brutality, dehumanization, and genocide is one of the worst in the world. Hundreds of thousands of Africans were raped, maimed, and killed over the course of the ravenous plundering of the Congo's natural resources.

The skulls were casually listed alongside paintings, coats, and other antiques. Human skulls. Of people. Imagine the Jeffrey Dahmer collection of skulls being sold on eBay? Or going to Arlington Cemetery digging up one hundred skulls of soldiers and placing them up for auction at Sotheby's as "history"? When we swap the nouns, these situations seem to become clearer.

Geneviève Kaninda, the coordinator of the Collective at Colonial Memory said it best, "It is simply a scandalous sale, it is a sale of the skulls of victims of colonization . . . This auction is a bit like killing them a second time in fact." She and many Belgians vocally condemned the sale, which ultimately led to it being canceled.

I'm glad the sale was stopped, but you have to wonder who thought this was an acceptable thing to do in the first place. How could people from a country so steeped in brutality even consider allowing any further profit from that brutality? How could they not learn from the past? It shows how deeply people are able to disconnect what they did from what they're doing.

It would be easy to sit on our side of the pond in judgment, but where are the places we disconnect old harms from modern-day practices?

ASK YOURSELF

- It's been said that tradition is peer pressure from dead people. How connected are you to your traditions? Do you feel a loss when asked to give up your traditions or artifacts? Why?
- What are the symbols/artifacts you hold most dear?
- In the United States there are deeply held traditions that have their roots in deeply troubling histories (i.e., Thanksgiving, Columbus Day). How do you reconcile the truth of these traditions with the normal ways they are celebrated? Should we change the traditions? Remove them? Disregard the new information?
- What is the cost of the loss of tradition?
- Do you expect people who migrate to a new country to give up their traditions and adopt the traditions of their new country? Why or why not?

Chapter 3

Replace Inadequate Language

"Words, he decided, were inadequate at best, impossible at worst.
They meant too many things. Or they meant nothing at all."
—PATRICIA A. MCKILLIP, *IN THE FORESTS OF SERRE*

I ONCE HEARD NOTED ASTROPHYSICIST NEIL DE GRASSE TYSON speak about the fallacy of our language. He said "The tide doesn't actually come in and out. What happens is, there is a bulge of water, two of them, on opposite sides of the Earth, caused by the Sun and the Moon, and Earth turns inside that bulge. So when we say the water rises and falls tidally, what's happening is we are rotating into the bulge and then out of the bulge. So the bulge is already there and all we do is pass through and the water gets high and it gets low. So we're stuck with language from our own perspective rather than the language of what's actually happening. It's simpler that way to say the water goes in and out."[39] In other words, the tide doesn't come in and out, the Earth goes in and out. He also said, "It's simpler to say the Sun sets, rather than Earth rotated such that our angle of view on this stationary Sun fell below our local horizon."

I was transfixed. What Neil taught me that day was world-changing. The sun doesn't set. Actually, the Earth sets. People all over the world gather each evening to watch what we all call a sunset. And it isn't true!

Our inherited language was faulty in large part because we centered our description of these natural phenomena around ourselves. In our language, we are the center of our universe.

Can you imagine all the ways this faulty understanding has shaped the world? How many experiments, inventions, and processes were based on this faulty understanding? How do you build a brilliant future on incorrect information?

We like to believe that we are intelligent people. We hope that when we get new information, we are eager to incorporate it into our understanding. But I don't think we're right about that. What would happen if I started a movement to change the term from sunset to earthset? Do you think people would care if earthset was more accurate? Do you think people would be eager to embrace this truth? Or do you think there would be immeasurable resistance? How many people would prefer the lie to the truth? How many would actively fight against the truth?

They would say things like:

It's always been this way.

Why do you hate our traditions?

We've been doing it this way too long to change.

It's too hard to change.

It will take too much to change it. There are more important things to focus on.

We don't love the truth as much as we think we do. All too often, our language becomes a cage of sorts because our language is a vehicle for history, values, beliefs, and culture. In the face of new realities, we can be hesitant to change our language to match.

WE NEED MORE WORDS

The Inuit people have over thirty words for snow.[40] If you live in a frozen tundra, snow is important. Whether it is wet, light, powdery, or an avalanche matters. We have only one word for racism. We use the same terminology to talk about a Klansman burning a cross on my lawn that we use for a guidance counselor telling all the Black and Brown kids not to bother applying to the elite schools because they don't stand a chance. Both are racist, but they are not the same.

We use the same word for that full spectrum of experience. And it's inadequate. We need more words. We need to build vocabulary that serves the complexity of the conversations we need to have. For example, if we care about racism, we will welcome a more thoughtful nuanced vocabulary around it, just like the Inuit.

We have inadequate language in every part of our society.

In the oil and gas sector, there is a real estate role called a "land man." A landman is an agent employed by an oil or gas company to secure leases of mineral rights and land for drilling. I remember meeting my first female land man, and the experience was jarring. Other falsely gendered words like *policeman* or *fireman* have a soft *a*. They also have alternative terms like *police officer* and *firefighter*. There is no alternative title to *land man* (at least so far).

Imagine how challenging it is to have an aspiration to a role that is so absolutely gendered? Imagine how many people tried to talk the few women out of the industry? Imagine the perpetual awkwardness. How do you introduce yourself? If you're like me, you're probably wondering why not just change the name? Well, I imagine it is like *earthset*. Our language is inherited. Once a concept is solidified in our minds, we can be extremely resistant to change.

Language both defines and confines us.

I remember doing a presentation about inclusion to an audience several years ago where I used the term "Eskimo." A member of the audience sent me a note informing me that the correct term was *Inuit*. The name "Eskimo" was actually a derogatory slur given to the Inuit people by White colonizers. I had no idea it was offensive. I replaced the term immediately.

Unfortunately, I've seen others react differently to such correction. They say things such as:

I'm too old to change.

I'll never remember to say it that way.

What's the big deal?

Everyone is so sensitive these days.

I've been saying that for years.

Does it really matter?

As we make room for the inclusion of new, better words, we must equally be committed to the purging of poor, harmful, or inartful ones.

Words make our world. By definition, language is reductionist. We don't have a word for EVERYTHING. You have to leave some things out. Consequently, you limit your ability to express certain concepts when you speak in only one language. This is why so many languages borrow concepts from other cultures like *mise en place*, *ikigai*, *siesta*, *déjà vu* or *hakuna matata*.

Take as an example the Swedish word *lagom*. Roughly translated, it means "enough." But not in the English way we say "enough" as in "barely enough" or "sufficient." It denotes being satisfied. Being full. There is a common phrase, "Lagom is as good as a feast." This means you can only eat as much as you can eat. Everything above what you can consume is superfluous. There is a point where you can achieve contentment. Anything beyond that is unnecessary. It's a beautiful concept we don't really have in English.

As we explore differences among us, we will definitely come across experiences for which we have no language, because we never noticed or named them before. We must stay open to, even welcoming of, that evolution.

The size of the goldfish is limited by the size of the bowl they live in. Does your language limit your growth?

WORDS ARE CHARGED

Language has been weaponized. What does it mean to be "professional"? "Christian"? "Masculine"? "Elite"?

Imagine you are hooked up to a blood pressure machine. Now read the following list out loud:

Proud Boys	Fascist
Black Lives Matter	Woke
Sex Worker	Civilized

Border Wall	The Thin Blue Line
Pronouns	Pro-Life
Socialism	Sexism
Incel	Racist
Christian Nationalist	Triggered
Snowflake	Cancel Culture
All Lives Matter	Elite
Evangelicals	Model Minority
#MeToo	Trans
Karen	Vaccinations
QAnon	Antifa
Zionist	Tech Bro
Drag Queen	Critical Race Theory
MAGA	Red Pill

If you're like most people, your blood pressure has ticked up just a bit. These words have become electric in our culture.

Bad actors often use the third rail because they know that's where the power is. These words have been coopted to derive power from triggering you. There are those who seek to monetize your outrage. It's important to understand that in some cases, words are even bastardized and manipulated to neuter them. How do we live and lead in a world without a shared truth? How do we communicate with each other if we don't have a shared meaning?

It's why I am very careful with jargon. It is critical to have a shared language. When people start having these difficult conversations, somebody throws out some language, whether it be *privilege, critical race theory* (CRT), *real American, affirmative action,* or *racism,* and everybody's triggered, because we don't have a shared understanding of what the phrases mean. We also don't know what meaning the person using them is trying to apply. So I want to caution you to be careful about language. Don't get hung up: focus on the intent, focus on that person's heart, focus on what the message is, and challenge yourself to not get stopped by inadequate language.

Willie Nelson famously said, "If you really want to get along with someone, let them be themselves." It can be challenging to have difficult conversations, because we can get offended by the tone or vocabulary being used. We need to be less concerned with the words used to fix broken things, and more concerned with fixing the broken things. If we agree that the language is imperfect and you struggle sometimes with the words, can we allow that for another person? Try to look past how they're saying something to make sure you understand what they're saying. For example, sometimes people come into a discussion with an angry, escalated tone, but what they really feel is fear. They're afraid you won't hear them, respect them or address their concerns. They may not trust you. You will not earn that trust by escalating to match their tone. You will earn it by listening deeply and offering solutions for the underlying concern.

One area of interaction that has a great deal of trouble with this is between police and citizens. There was a time when police were required to live in the neighborhoods they served. That is no longer the case and very often, police live in suburban (often predominantly White) areas and commute into inner-city areas to work. The more segregated these communities are from each other, the more difficult it can be to relate to one another. Different cultural groups have different communication styles. For example, when I deliver a keynote address to some groups, they will respond, cheer, talk back, and are generally expressive, while other groups sit in complete silence. I used to think the latter group was not enjoying the presentation, but then they would give a standing ovation at the end. Their vocalization or lack thereof was no indicator of their feelings. They were just different culturally.

This same phenomenon happens with police. They may come from communities that communicate in more low-key ways. On a scale from 1–10, they may talk to each other at a 2 or 3. But the communities of color they enter may communicate at a base level of 6. This is a terrible foundation for good communication, especially when power lies on only one side of the communication.

OFFICER (comes in at 3): "What seems to be the problem?"

CITIZEN TRIES TO EXPLAIN (at 6): "Something terrible is happening. You need to do something."

OFFICER (remaining at 3): "Ma'am. There's no need to yell."

CITIZEN (still at 6): "I'm not yelling. I'm just trying to tell you what's going on."

OFFICER (at 4): "You need to calm down."

CITIZEN (annoyed because they are not being helped, goes to 7): "You need to stop telling me to calm down and actually help with the problem."

OFFICER (jumps to 8 or 9): "You don't tell me what to do. I tell you what to do. If you don't calm down, you're gonna end up in cuffs."

And away we go. . . .

You get the idea. The officer perceives the citizen as angry or aggressive when they're not. The citizen perceives the officer as disinterested or dispassionate when they're not. The officer feels threatened unnecessarily and feels the need to escalate their tone in an effort to take control. But this rapid escalation from 3 to 8 is jarring and scary to the citizen. Scared people rarely have quality conversations.

As you have conversations with people who are different from you, it is important to keep these dynamics in mind and try to mitigate them whenever possible.

MEANINGS KEEP MOVING

Kevin, a Black manager, gathered his busy, time-constrained team for a meeting to generate solutions for a critical issue that had come up with their largest client. His team was bright and creative, and they offered up and discussed many ideas, but none really hit the mark. Ashley was a young White woman who hadn't been working with the team very long. She had a great idea but was hesitant to share it with so many senior performers. After listening to all the suggestions for over thirty minutes, she finally gathered the nerve to share her solution. Kevin listened, then said, "Say less. Let's get to work, people."

Kevin jumped back into his day's many tasks and was surprised when Tricia from human resources called him into an emergency meeting. When he arrived, he was shocked to see Ashley visibly upset and Tricia obviously displeased with him.

Tricia kicked off the meeting. "Kevin, we expect a minimum standard of respect between employees at this company. I don't understand why you would tell Ashley to shut up in front of a whole room full of team members. It's your job to develop new employees, not humiliate them."

Kevin had no idea what she was talking about. He had done no such thing. He would never tell a member of his team to shut up, and definitely not in front of anyone else. He turned to Ashley in confusion.

Ashley said, "I was just trying to help. If you didn't like my idea, you could have just picked another one, not tell me to shut up."

"But I loved your idea. That's why I told the team to get to work implementing it."

"You did not. You said 'Say less' and ended the meeting."

Suddenly, clarity dawned on Tricia and Kevin. When he had said "Say less" to Ashley, she interpreted it to mean "Shut up," rather than as an affectionate slang term that means "You don't even need to keep talking because I'm already sold on the idea." When Kevin heard Ashley's idea, the meeting could end because it was vastly superior to everyone else's.

Kevin said as much and Tricia turned to Ashely and asked if she had ever watched the movie *Jerry Maguire*, which she had. "Do you remember when the female lead said 'You had me at hello'?" Understanding washed over Ashley. That was a cultural reference she was familiar with. She had misunderstood the interaction completely. A younger person may not have even been familiar with the *Jerry Maguire* reference.

Language is always moving. Different colloquial terms emerge, pop culture references gain in popularity, and those differences can be enhanced between different racial, ethnic, and regional groups.

We have to take care in our use of this language. Clarity in communication takes work. It is essential that we are thoughtful about how our messages are being interpreted—or more importantly, misinterpreted—by the listener. Kevin could have said, "That's the idea I think we should go with." Sometimes slang or colloquialisms can be used to create comfort and familiarity within a team, but as in this situation, it can come at quite a cost.

We also have to take care in our interpretation. It is critical to slow down to confirm understanding as much as possible before taking offense. We often say we want people to be authentic, but are we putting in the work to understand them? Are we truly committed to processing these different communication styles?

Lastly, language is evolving (frustratingly). When we are the center, we can be frustrated by the constant evolution of inclusive language. Is it Hispanic or Latinx? Black or African American? Disabled or person with a disability? LGBT or LGBTQIA+? The inadequacy of our language should not stop us from communicating. Just the opposite. We should work harder to overcome the barriers to successfully living and working together.

DON'T BE AFRAID TO UPDATE

Because language is always moving, it is important to stay abreast of changes in language. We need to open to meaning shifting. For example, the following terms need to be updated:

Mankind → Humankind

Manpower → Workforce

Policeman → Police officer

Landlord → Property owner

Fireman → Firefighter

Congressman → Legislator, senator, representative

Chairman → Chair

Husband or wife → Spouse or partner

Words are always shifting and evolving in their meaning. Some groups will accept the shift, and some will reject it. That is the dynamic nature of language. Instead of being frustrated by it, we need to be committed to the learning process and understand that at times we will get it wrong. But that's just a part of the journey.

THE POWER TO NAME A THING

> *"And I saw what divided me from the world was not anything intrinsic to us, but the actual injury done by people intent on naming us, intent on believing that what they have named us matters more than anything we could actually ever do."*
>
> —TA-NEHISI COATES

Language is subjective. There is no greater power than the power to name a thing. We subjectively apply that power every day. In the difference between *scavenging* for food and *looting*. Why a man who can fly is *Superman*, but a woman who can fly is a *witch* (and we only burn one of them). Symbols are equally fickle. A hoodie is cool on a tech CEO, but an indicator of criminality on a Black teenager walking home in the rain. The subjective nature of our nomenclature shapes our experiences and attitudes.

Thug, gangbanger, wetback, cripple, spinster, ghetto, trailer trash, bimbo, slut, redneck, pansy, sissy, wuss, Karen . . . If we're not careful, words can limit worlds.

What's the difference between an *expat* and an *immigrant*? Why do we use phrases like *run like a girl* and *man up*?

What does it mean to be *professional*? Box braids are perceived as *unprofessional* until Kim Kardashian or Bo Derek wears them. Then they're *stylish*.

As we move through our world, we need to be more thoughtful about the ways our language drives our decision-making and our notions of what's possible. Any language that limits us should be removed. Our words matter.

ASK YOURSELF

- Do you ever refer to experiences or conditions as "ghetto," "backwoods," or "trailer trash"? What exactly do these terms mean?
- How quickly do you adapt to evolving language? Do you resist changes in language or readily embrace them? For example, some people, when informed that calling someone "retarded" is unacceptable, immediately cease use of that word. Others struggle and get frustrated when they are challenged for using it. Do you accept changes like this easily? Why or why not?
- How do you personally define the following words: *Racism, date rape, Karen, cancel culture, triggered, patriotism, snowflake, socialism, inclusion, privilege*? Where does your sense of these words come from?
- Do you ever feel like it is unsafe for you to speak? Do you fear offending people by saying the wrong thing or using the wrong terminology? How does that change your behavior?

Chapter 4

Reimagine Thoughtless Charity

"There comes a point where we need to stop just pulling people out of the river. We need to go upstream and find out why they're falling in."

—DESMOND TUTU

G ROWING UP IN THE FLATBUSH AREA OF BROOKLYN GAVE ME little opportunity to meet, let alone talk to, Native Americans. Haitians, Italians, Dominicans, Koreans, so many people from all over the world crossed my path in New York City, but never someone like him. And here he was sitting in front of me, brown, open, patient, and oddly regal. I met Cody Two Bears at a conference in Los Angeles. It was the kind of conference where the children of the 1 percent gather to pontificate about the problems facing the world and how they are uniquely positioned to solve them. They wrestled with the burden of their wealth as they discussed the future of edibles and NFTs over organic free-range chicken, vegan mushroom risotto, and kombucha. On this gorgeous sunny day, surrounded by privilege, we sat together. We sat and talked about his world. He answered me gently and with a candor that took my breath away. I was grateful, because I had a lifetime of questions.

Cody told me about life on the reservation. About his recent leadership at the Standing Rock protests. The United States has a perfect record of breaking treaties with Native American people. This latest assault was no exception.

The Standing Rock protests, also known as the Standing Rock Sioux Tribe's opposition to the Dakota Access Pipeline (DAPL), began in

2016 in response to the proposed construction of an oil pipeline that would pass through the Standing Rock Indian Reservation and cross under the Missouri River, which is the primary source of drinking water for the Standing Rock Sioux Tribe and millions of others downstream. The tribe and many supporters were concerned that a leak or spill could contaminate the water and damage sacred burial grounds and other culturally significant sites. The protests drew attention and support from Indigenous people and environmental activists from around the world and lasted for several months, with clashes between protesters and law enforcement.

Cody's life had been spent in constant defense. He had a very different story of America. We talked about death. Not just death from a distant past, but the lives that were currently being taken each year . . . by the cold.

He explained that, on the reservation, between three and ten people freeze to death in their homes each year, due to the instability of the power grid and lack of resources. The population of the reservation was smaller than the constellation of apartment buildings I grew up in. I couldn't imagine Ms. Jones in apartment 3C and the lovely couple in apartment 5J dying this way. But people from this community froze to death every year while sleeping in their beds.

I wasn't a stranger to death. Violence and sickness had taken many neighbors from me, but, at this point in our history, I couldn't imagine losing a handful of my community to the weather every year.

How did we even happen to meet? Like so many people of color, we bonded over disrespect. Earlier in the conference, we were randomly seated together at a table with ten others. The food and wine were flowing and the conversation was lively. Each person was interesting and notable in their own way, some by their own might and some by the heft of their family names. One of the White men at the table shared the fact that he had recently visited a reservation in Oklahoma. He had enjoyed watching some of their ceremonies, but he was disappointed that there were some rites he was not permitted to watch. Cody explained that some of the holiest of rites were private religious experiences restricted to tribal members only. This seemed to anger the guest, and caustically he said, "If you want us to help your people, it seems like you would be glad we are even interested and would just show us everything." The people of color at the table gasped.

These people, after giving so much, were expected to give even more. And in exchange for what? Help. Kindness. Charity.

As we sat alone in the sunshine talking about his world, Cody and I spoke about that awkward moment at the dinner. How familiar it was. The disingenuous offer of care and kindness in exchange for the low, low price of dignity and personhood. We talked about the odd practice of centering oneself in the middle of someone else's tragedy. How it felt to be reduced to a caricature, being seen only as a curiosity, not as a person.

I am usually a talkative person, but his stories silenced me. My few contributions to the conversation were questions. I asked him about how Native Americans were depicted on television, about treaties, about joy. With his gentle permission, I asked about alcoholism, education, and poverty on the reservation. But as we sat in an encampment of obscene wealth with the kale, goat yoga, and sound baths to prove it, I asked him about charity, and his words changed my view forever.

"People are waking up to the horrific treatment Native Americans have received in the United States. You must have so many people coming forward with offers to help."

He grimaced and said, "Yes, but we have to turn over 80 percent of those offers away."

I was stunned. 80 percent? Why on earth would you have to turn away so much kindness?

"People don't want to give you what you need," he said. "They want to give you what they need you to have."

Sometimes it's their failed prototype. Other times it's their defective inventory. They give you what they no longer want, their useless, broken things, in exchange for a photo op or a tax cut.

Sometimes what they give you is about them feeling good.

He was right about that. I remember after the brutal murder of twenty-seven people, including twenty first graders, at Sandy Hook Elementary, people sent 65,000 teddy bears to the suffering town.[41] So many were donated, in fact, that it became a full-time job to figure out what to do with them. As so often happens, their thoughtless gifts had become a chore.

A similar phenomenon happened in Houston after Hurricane Harvey. Record rainfall had displaced more than 30,000 people from their homes. The main shelter was the convention center downtown that housed 10,000 people. As the emergency shelter staff struggled to provide beds, food, and safety, they also had another struggle. Tens of thousands of pounds of clothing that had been "donated."

Now, this seems like a wonderful thing. Victims of the storm had lost everything. They needed replacement shoes and pants and night clothes. Some people generously donated those items. But unfortunately, others didn't. They donated graduation gowns and used underwear. Ski wear and bridesmaids' dresses. When they reached into their linen closet to find an item to donate, they did not reach for the items at the top, the ones they would use for their own children. They reached to the bottom to get the stained items with the holes. That is how they "helped." Instead of helping victims sift through the tatters of their lives destroyed by the storm, volunteers were sifting through the garbage people had sent masquerading as kindness.

I understood perfectly what Cody meant. He went on to say more. "The few that want to give you something useful, want to give it in a way that serves them, not you." They may give a big, complicated piece of machinery to generate electricity or irrigate crops, but they will not commit to its maintenance. They will not service it or teach anyone on the reservation to service it, so it works for a while, then breaks down.

The reservation is littered with such "gifts" from the past. "So I tell them no," he said. "I cannot have our children growing up in a graveyard of broken promises."

Thoughtless, self-serving, incomplete charity is not charity at all.

EMPATHY . . . SORTA

While growing up, I had a number of friends who would go on mission trips during spring break. They would travel to far-flung locales like Africa and Mexico to help the poor. It always struck me as odd. On their route to the airport, they passed through five poor neighborhoods. Why didn't any of them merit their mercy or attention? When did charity become a destination?

There is a patience and a mercy we often extend to people who are far away that we do not give to our neighbors. In this wealthy country, we assume they are in need because of some personal failing. But could it be something beyond their control? Maybe medical debt robbed them of their life savings. Or they grew up in food deserts with limited access to healthcare. When they don't have the right résumé or the right education, we say it's because they did not work hard, not because the average education now costs $100,000 even at a state school.

We can be tempted to help children because, after all, they are "innocent." But even how we do that is riddled with judgment.

I've always disliked the way we do holiday toy drives for the poor. Sometimes it's a guy in a Santa suit, sometimes not. Each child is given a gaily wrapped gift while the parent stands in the back, watching.

The parents are always grateful, but somehow diminished. Made smaller by their replacement as the hero in their child's life. Paying the electric bill and putting food on the table are necessary but weak competitors for a gaily wrapped gift.

I didn't like it, so I changed it. My kindness shouldn't center on me. I don't need to be the hero in your child's life. My family hosts an annual toy giveaway in poor neighborhoods here in Houston called the Good Givers. We partner with an apartment complex to identify the neediest families. One mother with five children had recently lost her husband to an aneurysm. Another family had suffered the death of all four grandparents to COVID. Some were just struggling to make ends meet, working low-paying jobs but loving their children as fiercely and completely as the rest of us do.

The selected parents are invited to come to a room where we have laid out hundreds of toys for them to pick from. From these, they choose the toys they think their child would enjoy. Together, we wrap the toys along with any batteries and supplies needed for the toy and send them on their way. It's a really special day we look forward to each year.

Now, before you nominate me for sainthood, allow me to share where my own bias reared its ugly head. As we planned this event, we struggled with what to do for the teenagers. You know teenagers are impossible to shop for even when you do know them, let alone when they are strangers. But teenagers are still children in the family who need kindness and encouragement. They are often overlooked, and we didn't want to do that.

My daughter suggested we give them gift cards. This is a perfectly reasonable idea and the normal gift for teenagers all over the country. But I am embarrassed to admit that I hesitated.

The first idea that ran through my head was pretty terrible. What if the teens never get their gift? What if the parents keep the gift cards? This is a particularly interesting question because it belies the truly unfair assumptions we have about people who are in need of help.

Why did I think that because people are poor, they must be deceptive or criminal? Why do we give the rich the perpetual, undeserved benefit of the doubt while micromanaging the poor at every turn? I knew better, but even I hesitated. Biases rarely give us up easily.

And what if they did use the gift card for another need? If they reallocate a resource I freely gave to them to a higher purpose or need than I was personally aware of, would that be so terrible? If they needed food on the table or to pay the electric bill so the heat would stay on, shouldn't I give them the respect to do so? Don't they have the autonomy to make choices for their own lives? Or do I always know better?

We need to be thoughtful about how we give. We must make sure that we allow for the dignity and humanity of those we are trying to assist. The toxic nature of an ill-conceived kindness is dehumanizing and an unexpected barrier to strong, Indivisible teams.

THE PERILS OF PITY

"The wait for a table will be about forty minutes."

We were hungry and tired from a long day of training, but the food smelled so good and we were too fried to go anywhere else. We looked around to find a seat but there were none to be found. This was fine, I thought, for most of our group, but what about John?

My friend John Register is the nicest guy you will ever meet. He is an incredible encourager and friend. As a dynamic keynote speaker, he focuses on leadership and resilience. He also happens to only have one leg. His leg was amputated over twenty years following an accident. Since then, he has thrived despite this injury.

As we stood in the restaurant's crowded lobby, I became concerned. Wanting him to be comfortable, I sought out a manager to ask for a chair for him. After some fuss, one was produced and brought to John. Unfortunately, the staff had made a spectacle. Every eye in the waiting room was on him. Needless to say, he refused the chair.

I instantly regretted my decision. I had inserted myself, calling attention where none was required. Here was this strong man, an actual Paralympian, that I was infantilizing with my "help." Also, John is a gentleman. There was no way he would sit while the five women he was waiting with were standing. I was just totally wrong.

I wondered how often I was wrong. How often my "help" was unnecessary and even harmful? How many times had my underestimation robbed someone of their maximum potential? We all struggle with ableism. Ableism is discrimination or prejudice against individuals with disabilities. It can take many forms, including physical barriers in the built environment, and in my case, attitude-based discrimination. Ableism can also refer to the societal belief that being disabled is inherently bad or inferior.

People with disabilities have been underestimated powerfully throughout history. According to the US Census Bureau, in 2019, an estimated 61 million people in the United States, or 19 percent of the population, had a disability. That number may be an underestimation as not all disabilities are visible or reported. COVID-19 likely resulted in 1.2 million more disabled people by the end of 2021.[42]

According to the Bureau of Labor Statistics, the unemployment rate for people with disabilities was 9.2 percent in 2019, which is significantly higher than the overall unemployment rate of 3.7 percent for that year.[43] However, it's worth noting that this data might not be completely accurate as not all disabilities are reported or visible.

In recent years, the opportunities for remote work have increased. This has led to a decrease in unemployment among people with disabilities. This lets us know that when opportunities for full participation are created, this chronically underestimated population is able to contribute and thrive.

•

It is wrong to trap people with low expectations. There are many members of our society who have the capacity to participate in incredible, even genius, ways. With the smallest amount of sensitivity, we can unlock the potential of so many talented people. And we need their talents. We need their contributions.

When we solve for groups that are experiencing challenges, there's always a multiplier effect for everyone. Take the curb-cut phenomenon. This refers to the idea that design features created to improve accessibility for people with disabilities (such as curb cuts, or ramped edges of sidewalks, that allow wheelchairs to roll over them), can also benefit people who don't have disabilities, like parents with strollers, cyclists, or delivery workers with hand trucks. The idea is that these design features are not just helpful for a specific group but can benefit society as a whole, and promote inclusiveness and accessibility for everyone.

Whenever we create policies and procedures that are sensitive to groups that are being challenged by our current practices, there are almost always additional benefits. By supporting some, we help all.

ASK YOURSELF

- In the past, have you thought of being inclusive as kindness or charity? Do you think of inclusion as being in your best interests or as something "nice to do" for someone else?
- List the last five charitable donations you made, who they were for, how it helped, and how you could've helped more effectively.
- How can you transform your gifts into impact? In the past, you may have donated to a scholarship drive, but to uplevel that, maybe you could join a parent-teacher organization and volunteer or adopt a classroom at a low-performing school in your area. Maybe you have donated old, discarded furniture after a home remodel, but think how impactful it would be to buy brand-new bunk beds for a single mother living in a small apartment.
- What opportunities do you hoard for the benefit of your children at the expense of others?

Chapter 5

Process Unresolved Grief

"I sat with my anger long enough, until she
told me her name was grief."

—GINA BRENNA BUTZ

HE RAISED ME.

Like so many single mothers, my mom worked two jobs to care for my brothers and me. She often worked nights, which meant we were home alone a lot. And we watched TV. There were many fantastic characters. Some made us laugh and some made us cry, but there was one above all others that taught us. His name was Dr. Heathcliff Huxtable. He was a doctor and his wife, Claire, was an attorney. Their large family lived in a beautiful brownstone in Brooklyn, New York.

And he was Black.

But not Black in any way I had ever seen on television before. He wasn't drug-dealer Black or pimp Black or gangbanger Black. He was a smart, professional, loving father and doting husband. I was transfixed.

And I was not alone. *The Cosby Show* grew to be the most-watched show from 1985 to 1989. It became "must-see" TV. At its peak, the show averaged thirteen million viewers per episode in real time. There were no streaming services. There was no on-demand television. If you wanted to see it, you had to be there. And we wouldn't dare miss it, because the next day at school, everyone would be talking about what Vanessa did or how funny Theo was. The whole world was fascinated.

Each week, Dr. Huxtable taught us something new. One episode was about curfews. Another was about money. Yet another would be about the importance of HBCUs. Between *The Cosby Show* and its spin-off, *A Different World*, he single-handedly persuaded a generation to go to college.

He taught us pride and patience, jazz and art, the power of strong families, and the rewards a commitment to excellence could provide. Even children who were not allowed to watch television were made to watch *The Cosby Show*.

He was everybody's father. And he was perfect.

Dr. Huxtable won my heart, but Bill Cosby broke it.

What had begun in whispers leapt to the front of every newspaper.

"Women Come Forward to Accuse Bill Cosby"

"Bill Cosby Accused of Drugging Women"

"Cosby's Sexual Assault Rumors"

I didn't want to believe it. How could it be true? In a world where so few Black men get to be heroes, why were people attacking mine? Like so many others, I rejected it. A person who could do so much good couldn't possibly be so bad.

But the rumors became charges. The allegations became indictments. One woman became three. Three became nine. Nine became twenty. It felt like each day brought a new allegation. Women were finding the courage to come forward to tell us how he drugged them and sexually assaulted them. The total number of women who have come forward is sixty. Who knows who still remains in the shadows?

I am a lover of truth. But this truth was too hard. Sometimes our heroes let us down.

As a woman who has experienced the unwanted attention of men all my life, I know the courage it took for those women to come forward. I know how it feels to not be believed because your value is perceived as less than that of your aggressor. I know what it's like for the world to demand you forgive their beloved yet unrepentant offender. I want women to be believed. I want men who create harm to be brought to justice.

But, I also loved him.

Change, even when positive, can create grief. Eventually, I had to separate the man from the message, the fiction from the fact. There was grief associated with the disassembling of my story. There are many stories being disassembled right now and their loss triggers sadness to which we don't always feel entitled. But if we want to move forward, we have to learn to leave the past.

The Cajuns have a saying. "Every person needs to know how to throw a funeral." Translation: You have to learn to bury the dead, no matter how beloved or precious.

NO ONE CARES ABOUT THE WHITE GUY

To do this work, we have to keep reaching out to meet people where they are. I was once brought in to work with a leadership team that had set a goal of being 40 percent women and people of color in five years. At the time, the leadership team had fifteen members, thirteen of whom were White men. Their employee base was almost 70 percent women and 45 percent people of color. I wish I could say that they had come to this moment of enlightenment out of the goodness of their hearts, but the truth is, they were being hammered on company review sites like Glassdoor, and their recruitment efforts were starting to struggle.

Before I went in to speak to them, the C-suite leader who brought me in warned me to expect resistance and even hostility to what I had to say. It would not have been the first time. In many organizations I work with, I am the first DEI professional they have ever brought in.

I started the meeting by building trust and rapport. I asked them about their work, their proudest achievements, and what they saw as the challenges facing their organization. I asked them about their families and their values. I then asked the question, "What do you think about this ambitious diversity goal?"

One gentleman answered quickly and transparently, obviously angry. He said, "It's a great idea in theory, but it means I have to get up. There are only so many seats. I was the last one added. To add them,

I have to give up my seat [at the leadership table]. No one cares that I have to get up."

Without missing a beat, I looked him directly in his eyes and said, "I care." I spent the next few minutes listening, giving space for the grief, the frustration, the disappointment. Then I asked him the hardest question of the session. "When you were invited to join this leadership team, you knew that the organization was overwhelmingly female, but they only had one woman on the board. You knew that it was almost half people of color, but there was only one Black person on the board." I asked him, "Did you care about them?"

And he had to admit that he didn't. He wanted us to understand his grief when by his own admission, he hadn't cared about anyone else's. That day, he moved from a 2 to a 4, and I celebrated his growth. He was able to anchor the proposed solution in his own values. While he was not thrilled about the sacrifice he personally might have to make, he could see that he had been largely unaware of the denied opportunities to the other employees in the organization. He believed in fairness, but had not really considered the unfairness experienced by others around him.

If we bring optimistic, jargon-free, possibility-laden solutions to the table, change is possible. With the right thinking and the right tools, anyone can change. We are capable of more than we think.

Throughout my years doing this work, there has been a great focus on helping marginalized populations navigate environments that are not inclusive and are sometimes toxic. This always struck me as odd because these populations generally do not have the authority to change these environments. What if the energy shifted from the management of their response to harm to the actual removal of the harm? What if instead of pushing women and minorities to get mentorship to adapt and navigate the pathology, we encouraged, even required, leaders to change it?

WHAT CHANGE FEELS LIKE

I am what I like to call "microfiche old," which means I'm old enough to remember the transition to the technology-powered movement of today. I remember when desktop computers replaced secretaries and executive assistants. Most companies were supportive of the changes. You could take five Microsoft Excel or Word classes a day. There was no shortage of training. But every organization came to a point where you were expected to write your own emails and create your own spreadsheets if you wanted to be a part of the future of the company.

I remember the complaints. The gripes. The actual physical pain experienced by those who just could not seem to adapt to this change. There was a grief. But the time came that you either adapted to this change or you were managed out of the company. To some, this felt harsh and unforgiving, not unlike the grief I see today, where people are being asked to learn the skills of navigating difference. As leaders, we have the responsibility to give as much support and as many tools as possible to facilitate the mastery of these skills. We must also be ready to manage the grief of those who are unwilling to do so and manage them out when necessary.

People fear change. That fear can sometimes block them from even trying. As Lucius Seneca said, "We are often more frightened than hurt; and we suffer more from imagination than in reality." We cannot allow fear to rob us of possibility.

YOU MUST REPLACE YOUR DEVILS

> When an impure spirit comes out of a person, it goes through arid places seeking rest and does not find it. Then it says, "I will return to the house I left." When it arrives, it finds the house unoccupied, swept clean, and put in order. Then it goes and takes with it seven other spirits more wicked than itself, and they go in and live there. And the final condition of that person is worse than the first. That is how it will be with this wicked generation.
>
> —MATTHEW 12:43–45 (NIV)

When your old stories, heroes, and beliefs are cleared out, they're not immediately replaced with nice ideas. You can feel empty, lost. Unresolved grief is the equivalent of the empty house in the verse above. When the demons were exorcized, they left an emptiness. Nothing replaced them.

I have seen this in my work more times than I care to share:
- People find the courage to call out racism among their friends and suddenly find themselves with no friends.
- LGBTQ+ people finally tell their families their truth and find themselves with no family.
- Executives take on the discriminatory practices in their companies and get labeled social justice warriors not concerned about the bottom line, and isolated from their peers.

This story plays out over and over again. When you find the courage to change, not everyone will come with you. You will never be more vulnerable than in this season. Anger and disillusionment are fertile soil for conspiracy theories and cynicism. Uncertainty is uncomfortable. You cannot allow more demons to move into the clean new space. You must learn to differentiate between the sound of your intuition guiding you and your traumas leading you.

Remember, you are in the midst of growth. There is no such thing as a "cater-fly." You have to allow the transition from caterpillar to butterfly. If you open a chrysalis in the midst of metamorphosis, it is a gooey, terrible mess. That's because the process is not complete. We are often too impatient to allow authentic, complete transformation to happen.

There is a fatigue that comes with loss. Change is exhausting. Right now we are in that stage of metamorphosis where we are the mushy, unrecognizable mess. Change and loss of our stories can feel brutal, but if we stop now, we will never fly.

ASK YOURSELF

- Are there changes that sadden you or make you uncomfortable? I challenge you to dig deep and really explore how you are processing the changes that are happening around you. You cannot address what you're unwilling to face. Examples: Technology, interracial marriage, remote work, artificial intelligence, increased publicity of transgender people, decline of small towns, rise of atheism, etc.

- All change needs to be managed. As human beings, we use simplicity and categorization to organize our reality and simplify our worlds. Our resistance to change is biological. We must effectively manage the process of addressing change and the emotions that especially rapid change can create. Harvard Business School outlines five steps for effective change management. Select one change that you are struggling with and use this model to create your plan of approach.

  1) Prepare the organization for change.
  2) Craft a vision and plan for change.
  3) Implement the changes.
  4) Embed changes within company culture and practices.
  5) Review progress and analyze results.*

- Is there any activity you previously enjoyed that feels no longer appropriate?

- Are there terms you used to use that you don't use anymore?

- How do you feel when you see films or TV shows from your childhood that you now see had inappropriate messaging?

---

* Kelsey Miller, "5 Critical Steps in the Change Management Process," *Business Insights*, Harvard Business School Online, March 19, 2020, https://online.hbs.edu/blog/post/change-management-process.

Part 2

BE AN OWNER, NOT A RENTER

Chapter 6

Give and Take

"People who use other people as stepping stones
will one day lose their balance."

—UNKNOWN

THE LAST TIME CINDY HAD SEEN HER HUSBAND CRY WAS WHEN she walked down the aisle to him on their wedding day. Mike was a buttoned-up guy who normally kept his emotions to himself. Today, they sat at the top of the stairs to the second floor and watched the water rise, the tears flowed freely. As the flood water rose, he was overwhelmed by its destructive power.

The rain continued to fall and wash away the home they had built together.

They did not have flood insurance. Why would they? Their house had never flooded before. Not in the six years they had lived there or in the twenty-three years Mike's father had lived there before them. During the storm, they fought their way around the house trying to save wedding albums, passports, and heirlooms like the letter his mom had written him on her deathbed: the precious pieces of their life. After the storm, they began the grueling work of picking up the bigger pieces.

At first, Mike and Cindy thought they had fallen victim to climate change, that rising sea levels and changing storm patterns had robbed them of their home. But in the weeks to come, they would learn that the devastation they faced was man-made in an entirely different way. Their home had been destroyed because of irresponsible development.

There was a housing boom in their city. Neighboring plots of land had been constructed in such a way that they had changed the floodplain. They had redirected the path water would take in the event of a storm: to Mike and Cindy's neighborhood.

Now, the obvious question one might have is, why didn't they sue someone? The answer? The city pointed the finger at the developers, and the developers were gone. They had sold their interests and extracted maximum profit from their projects, then moved on to their next community. They were long gone. After all, this wasn't their community.

These developers were takers. Unfortunately, they are not the only ones.

In 1961, during his inaugural address, John F. Kennedy admonished the nation. He said, "Ask not what your country can do for you, but what you can do for your country." It was a powerful challenge to those enjoying the fruits of America to contribute to the American experience rather than simply focusing on personal gain. While his words have stood the test of time, the sentiment has taken a beating. There are those among us who have picked up the mantle of taker rather than giver. People who are focused on their personal success with little concern for the cost to others around them.

- Superstores move into small towns, killing most of the businesses and thus the economy.
- People think they are smart if they can hide assets offshore to avoid paying their fair share of taxes.
- Some of our wealthiest corporations keep their workers below the threshold of full-time work to avoid paying for health insurance.
- Companies lay off employees not because of poor performance but to improve shareholder value.
- Our social media companies have turbocharged the circulation of damaging misinformation, sometimes even impacting our democracy.

- Pharmaceutical companies have addicted millions to opioids, all in the pursuit of wealth.

We have some takers among us.

We are heirs to a legacy that is in need of our attention. It is not perfect, but it is ours. You don't inherit the assets without the liabilities. If you inherit a beautiful old house, you inherit the crooked door frames and the rusty plumbing. You don't burn down the house. You fix the problems and you are grateful for them, because you have a house you didn't have to build.

Unfortunately, we often act more like renters than owners.

Owners care about long-term strength and viability. Renters utilize a space for their personal use and focus only on the time they will be in the property. In other words, owners fix the plumbing and the foundation. Renters use peel-and-stick tile.

I have never been to Japan, but I was scrolling, as one does, on social media and came across several stories about children taking the train to school by themselves. I must have watched thirty stories because I was so fascinated with the practice. Children as young as six years old were walking to the train station, waiting by themselves, boarding the train, transferring train lines, and then walking to school. All without incident. It felt impossible.

One train line has the practice of requiring the youngest children to wear yellow hats. This is done so the adults around them know to make themselves available if the child should need some assistance. The adults help children they do not know and have no visible connection to. But, in fact, they do have a connection. They are part of a community responsible to and for one another.

When the community comes together, what sounds impossible can become commonplace.

We've done it here before. When scientists Frederick Banting and Charles Best discovered insulin, they wanted to make it readily accessible to the world. They sold their patent rights for $1 each in an effort to keep this life-saving treatment affordable for everyone with diabetes. Today, the cost of insulin is out of reach for approximately one-third of people with diabetes.[44] The price of this hundred-year-old drug has tripled in the last decade alone. The formula hasn't changed. The people who wield it have.

THE DIFFERENCE BETWEEN OWNERS AND RENTERS

Our mentality has to shift. We act more like renters extracting temporary value rather than owners committed to long-term viability.

If you saw yourself as an owner, you would do everything in your power to make sure every child in America received a quality education. A renter just makes sure their kids get an education.

If you were the owner, you would do everything in your power to provide mental health care services and drug treatment services to address the problem of homelessness. A renter just wants the homeless moved out of sight.

To an owner, it would be a horrific emergency that a US city didn't have clean drinking water. A renter shakes his head and says, "What a shame" when these stories come across their timeline. It's sad to read stories of what's happening to "those" people over there.

Political gridlock would be unacceptable.

Guns could never be the number one cause of death of schoolchildren. Not on your watch.

An owner solves the problems. A renter kicks them down the road for someone else to tackle another day.

An owner is clear on the gifts America has provided them. They are clear about the ways they have benefited and want to prove worthy of those opportunities.

Take Harvard University, for example. As one of the best universities in the world, it attracts the best and brightest students in the country. Outperforming the competition to attend is virtually impossible. Harvard accepts 3.4 percent of their 57,000 annual applicants.

But why? Harvard's endowment is in excess of $53 billion. If their goal is to educate the best and brightest students, why not expand the number of students they serve? The caliber of their applicant pool is outstanding and attendance at such a school is life-changing for students who are afforded the opportunity. Why not expand the campus or create satellite campuses in other cities in the United States to allow more students to attend?

The 2022 freshman class at Harvard was 1,200 students; 36 percent of these were legacy admissions, meaning they were accepted not necessarily because they outpaced the competition, but because a parent or grandparent was an alum.

It feels like an institution that has received so much from America (its laws and policies, its philanthropy, its support) could give back a bit more. Instead, it has become the Birkin bag of higher education. Rare, elusive, and scarce. More luxury brand than partner in the building of America's future.

It's easy to pick on Harvard, but this phenomenon occurs in so many places in our society. The minimum wage has been $7.25 since 2009. The employees of some of our largest and wealthiest employers have to be supported by taxpayers with food stamps and public assistance. People vote against programs like Head Start and providing free school lunches to hungry children.

Something has to give. We must act in our own best interest. Remember, we're saving our own lives. We must scale our strengths on behalf of our broader community to secure our future. We need more owners.

Greed is a driver for many takers, but apathy is an equally destructive motivator.

For example, I live in Houston, Texas, where the population is approximately 2.5 million people. In the 2019 mayoral election, fewer than 200,000 people voted. These nonvoters are not bad people. They are people who just need to be reminded of their power. That they are not guests here. That they matter.

Luke 12:48 says, "To whom much is given, much is required," but I fear far too many have a winners-take-all mentality that cheats each new generation out of the promise enjoyed by the previous ones. Like the hedge funds and real estate companies that are buying up real estate all over the country and locking out first-time home buyers, too many are cannibalizing the American dream. We need more people to plant trees they will never sit under, and we need them now.

STOP DANCING WITH DYSFUNCTION

"Being good at thinking can make you worse at rethinking."
—ADAM GRANT

A friend of mine has been a renter all of her life and finally got the opportunity to buy her first home. She has a notoriously brown thumb. Knowing this about herself, she bought a townhouse that has virtually no grass outside. But she does have one tree. It's a giant tree that provides shade to not just her but her neighbors to the left and right. The mature trees in her neighborhood are what makes the real estate desirable, but that beauty comes at a cost. The roots of the trees have lifted the sidewalks all over the neighborhood. Joggers and dog walkers are relegated to the street because the sidewalks are so uneven. In their quest for survival, the roots of her massive tree have lifted the staircase leading up to the entrance of her townhouse. This has changed the pitch of the staircase, making it steep and, admittedly, a little dangerous. She even began warning women who were coming to visit to wear flat shoes so they didn't slip down the stairs. Her biggest fear was that someone would seriously hurt themselves. Her risk of being sued went up the longer the problem persisted. Like me, she grew up as a city slicker. She knows nothing about trees and roots and horticulture. She knows even less about stairs and their construction, but she is the owner of this house and, as such, the responsibility of addressing the problem falls to her.

Watching her struggle with this situation was enlightening. Owners should fix problems, but they don't always. They can have many reasons why:

They don't notice the problem: Chances are the pitch on the stairs was probably off when she bought the house. But because of her lack of familiarity with the area, she didn't notice.

They don't make the time to fix the problem: We all get consumed with the day-to-day activities in our lives, and even important issues can fall to the bottom of a too-full to-do list.

They minimize the impact of the problem: It can be easy to explain away the seriousness of the issue.

They have learned to adapt to the problem: We learn to dance with dysfunction by creating odd workarounds rather than repairing the situation.

They don't know how to fix the problem: The powerlessness of not having the skills or knowledge to address a problem can be paralyzing. Sometimes we don't even know who to call for help.

They feel like they can't afford to fix the problem: We often make the mistake of avoiding the short-term pain of investment, underestimating the exposure to long-term damage, even destruction.

•

The work of protecting our greatest assets is in fact work. We must push past distraction, inconvenience, and discomfort to make the sacrifices necessary to create optimal conditions. Delay is expensive and deferred attention can allow our gifts to slip away, sometimes unnoticed.

It takes courage to fix things.

Chapter 7

Make Peace With History

"Only when we are brave enough to explore our darkness will we discover the infinite power of our light."

—BRENÉ BROWN

IN 1931, DR. CORNELIUS RHOADS, A HARVARD-TRAINED ONCOLO-gist, was sent to Puerto Rico by the Rockefeller Institute soon after Hurricane San Felipe to study anemia and its effects on the population there. He had trained at Harvard, presumably learning the best methods of treatment for the patients he served. However, when he got to Puerto Rico, those standards were abandoned. A scandal erupted when a letter he had written was discovered, in which he asserted that he would withhold treatment from his patients just to see what would happen. He intentionally infected patients. He even referred to them as experimental animals.

Unfortunately, Rhoads was not the only doctor of his time whose racism led to the mistreatment of his patients. But the contents of a letter he wrote to colleagues back on the mainland revealed the depths of his hate and villainy.

Dear Ferdie:

The more I think about the Larry Smith appointment the more disgusted I get. Have you heard any reason advanced for it? It certainly is odd that a man out with the Entire Boston group, fired by Wallach and as far as I know, absolutely devoid of any scientific reputation, should be given the place.

I can get a damn fine job here and am tempted to take it. It would be ideal except for the Puerto Ricans—they are beyond doubt the dirtiest, laziest, most degenerate, and thievish race of men ever inhabiting this sphere. It makes you sick to inhabit the same island with them. They are even lower than Italians. What the island needs is not public health work, but a tidal wave or something to totally exterminate the population. It might then be livable. I have done my best to further the process of extermination by killing off 8 and transplanting cancer into several more. The latter has not resulted in any fatalities so far. The matter of consideration for the patients' welfare plays no role here—in fact, all physicians take delight in the abuse and torture of the unfortunate subjects

Do let me know if you hear any more news.

Sincerely, Dusty

(From How to Hide an Empire by Daniel Immerwahr, 144)[45]

Can you imagine being the research assistant who found this letter lying on the desk as you came in to do your work to help people? Can you imagine the outrage of the Puerto Rican people once this letter was made public? The governor, who had been appointed by the mainland, conducted an investigation and came across another letter even worse than this one. This unelected leader refused to release it and eventually cleared Rhoads.

Most of us would have been arrested, but Cornelius Rhoads didn't even get fired. The governor's finding was that, despite his written confession, Rhoads had not killed any Puerto Ricans. Rhoads did not deny writing the letter but claimed that it was merely a "parody" written for his personal amusement.

Wrapped in the credibility of the Rockefeller Institute and his Harvard degree, Rhoads returned to New York and was promoted to vice president of the New York Academy of Medicine. When World War II began, he became a colonel in the Army and became chief medical officer in the Chemical Warfare Service. He tested poison gas on 60,000 uniformed American soldiers, many of them (coincidentally?) Puerto Rican. These men had no idea that as they were conducting practice drills on San Jose Island, they were also being systematically poisoned by Dr. Rhoads.

For this work he was awarded the Legion of Merit in 1945.

His years of experience with chemical agents led him to believe that mustard gas could be used to treat cancer, so he took some of the remaining chemical weapons to test his theory. He then went on to become the first director of the world-renowned Sloan Kettering Institute. This work is the foundation of much of the cancer research we have today.

His cruelty was forgotten. His racism was erased. His reputation was polished and repackaged in cooperation with the prestigious entities that had endorsed and funded him. Their credibility was now inextricably linked to his. They needed him to be good, so he was.

So Rhoads was remembered as a hero. A savior. He was on the cover of *Time* magazine, and one of the world's most prestigious awards for cancer research was given in his name for over twenty years.

This man was made a hero.

But the truth came out. A Puerto Rican researcher connected with the association conferring the award and revealed the painful truth of Dr. Rhoads's story. And they listened. The name of the award was changed. I count this as a profound victory because it is often harder to accept a hard truth than it is to release a beloved lie. They made peace with history.

This example is a powerful one because the community that was challenged to make this change is relatively small. The story of Dr. Rhoads is not widely known. The association could have ignored the even smaller community asking them to make the change. But they didn't. There was discussion. There was disagreement. But they navigated the resistance to ultimately do the right thing.

These are the opportunities we all have in front of us. The opportunities to make changes in our associations, our schools, our clubs, our teams. The willingness to evolve. To be better when you know better. We all have the ability to do that every day.

Humankind produces more information now in an hour than we once did in a thousand years. As we learn more about our leaders, we are forced to confront hard truths that have been foundational in our development. While there is much to celebrate, there is also much to acknowledge and remediate. People love their stories, and there can be significant resistance to changing those stories even in the face of new information. We have every tool at our fingertips to know better. But knowing better isn't the same as doing better.

Fear of change can limit our progress forward. But we cannot allow it to. We shouldn't be afraid of past mistakes. We should be afraid of making them again.

We have many tragic mistakes in our past:

Slavery: Historians have estimated that 6 to 7 million enslaved people were imported to the New World during the eighteenth century alone, depriving the African continent of some of its healthiest and ablest men and women. Within several decades of being brought to the American colonies, Africans were stripped of human rights and enslaved as chattel, an enslavement that lasted more than two centuries.[46]

Trail of Tears: At the beginning of the 1830s, nearly 125,000 Native Americans lived on millions of acres of land in Georgia, Tennessee, Alabama, North Carolina, and Florida—land their ancestors had occupied and cultivated for generations. But by the end of the decade, very few natives remained anywhere in the southeastern United States. Working on behalf of White settlers who wanted to grow cotton on the Indians' land, the federal government forced them to leave their homelands and walk hundreds of miles to a specially designated "Indian Territory" across the Mississippi River.[47]

Women left out of the Constitution: In the early days of the United States, women were not allowed to own property unless they were single, widowed, or divorced. The Married Women's Property Acts were state laws in the United States that gave married women the right to own and control property in their own name. These laws were passed in the late nineteenth century, with the first one being passed in 1839 in New York. However, it wasn't until the end of the nineteenth century and the early twentieth century that most states in the United States passed such laws. The 19th Amendment to the US Constitution, which was ratified in 1920, granted women the right to vote. With the passing of the Married Women's Property Acts in the late nineteenth century, married women were granted the right to own and control property in their own name. This included the ability to open bank accounts and have checkbooks in their own name. However, even with these laws in place, women still faced discrimination and barriers when trying to access financial services. It wasn't until the passing of the Equal Credit Opportunity Act of 1974 and the Civil Rights Act of 1964 that discrimination against women in access to credit and financial services was made illegal.[48]

Chinese Exclusion Act: In the spring of 1882, the Chinese Exclusion Act was passed by Congress and signed by President Chester A. Arthur. This act provided an absolute ten-year ban on Chinese laborers immigrating to the United States. For the first time, federal law proscribed entry of an ethnic working group on the premise that it endangered the good order of certain localities.[49]

Japanese internment: Japanese internment camps were established during World War II by President Franklin D. Roosevelt through his Executive Order 9066. From 1942 to 1945, it was the policy of the US government that people of Japanese descent, including US citizens, would be incarcerated in isolated camps. Enacted in reaction to the Pearl Harbor attacks and the ensuing war, the incarceration of Japanese Americans is considered one of the most atrocious violations of American civil rights in the twentieth century.[50]

Turning away Jews fleeing the Holocaust: World War II prompted the largest displacement of human beings the world has ever seen—although today's refugee crisis is starting to approach its unprecedented scale. But even with millions of European Jews displaced from their homes, the United States had a poor track record offering asylum. Most notoriously, in June 1939, the German ocean liner *St. Louis* and its 937 passengers, almost all Jewish, were turned away from the Port of Miami, forcing the ship to return to Europe. More than a quarter of the ship's passengers died in the Holocaust.[51]

These are just a few practices that we look back on with shame. Some look at these failures as proof of the duplicity of America. They are disheartened by the disappointing choices made in our history. I see them differently. I see them as proof of the promise. We can look at the evidence of our fallibility or we can see these events as evidence of our ability to change, our power to amend, our power to be better together. We cannot allow hopelessness and helplessness to keep us from our duty. Change isn't accidental. It requires sheer will. Discouragement is a major impediment to forward progress. Many others have done the work of change. Things are better. We are far from perfect, but we have the power and the responsibility to keep making the story of America true. It's better because someone did the work.

Now it is our turn.

LET THE STORY CHANGE

A geologist shared a story with me. Her mentor, also a geologist, was once deployed to a work site by helicopter. When she arrived, she was not permitted to get off the helicopter to do her work because she was a woman. That was twenty years ago and would not happen today. Why? Because many people have worked tirelessly throughout the years to normalize the presence of women in many industries they were previously excluded from.

We have a ways to go, but it's important to look at what we have achieved in the last twenty years. Looking back, not letting her off the helicopter sounds ridiculous. But I ask you, what will we look back on twenty years from now? What common practice of today will seem ridiculous then?

In my lifetime, I have seen an incredible change. The rise in support for same-sex marriage has been especially dramatic over the last few decades. It went from 11 percent approval in 1988 to 71 percent in 2022.[52] This shift in public opinion has been driven by a variety of factors. Shows like *Ellen* and *Will & Grace* have increased visibility and acceptance of members of the LGBTQ community. Being able to actually see more gay relationships has changed attitudes toward marriage and family. Court decisions and legislative action at the state and federal levels have also played a role in shaping public opinion on this issue.

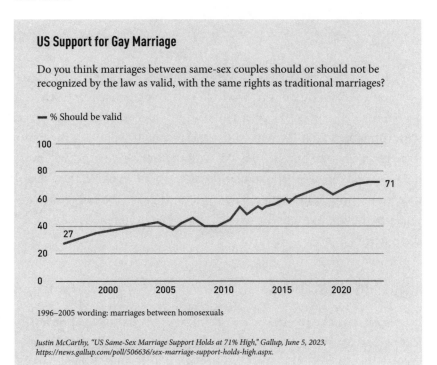

US Support for Gay Marriage

Do you think marriages between same-sex couples should or should not be recognized by the law as valid, with the same rights as traditional marriages?

— % Should be valid

1996–2005 wording: marriages between homosexuals

Justin McCarthy, "US Same-Sex Marriage Support Holds at 71% High," Gallup, June 5, 2023, https://news.gallup.com/poll/506636/sex-marriage-support-holds-high.aspx.

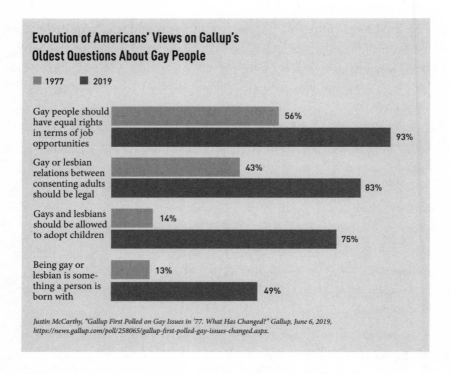

Evolution of Americans' Views on Gallup's Oldest Questions About Gay People

■ 1977   ■ 2019

Gay people should have equal rights in terms of job opportunities
56%
93%

Gay or lesbian relations between consenting adults should be legal
43%
83%

Gays and lesbians should be allowed to adopt children
14%
75%

Being gay or lesbian is something a person is born with
13%
49%

Justin McCarthy, "Gallup First Polled on Gay Issues in '77. What Has Changed?" Gallup, June 6, 2019,
https://news.gallup.com/poll/258065/gallup-first-polled-gay-issues-changed.aspx.

We are confronting our myths with new revelations, new truths, on an almost daily basis. Barely a day goes by that we aren't confronted with revelations that force us to try and reconcile what we now know to be true, what we have witnessed, with the stories we have held most dear—about fairness, about meritocracy, about equal rights, about race and immigration, rule of law, and on it goes. The old stories are breaking down, and good riddance, but what stories will we replace them with?

A MORE PERFECT UNION

People often make the mistake of thinking that you have to be a perfect person to create a perfect union. I am grateful this is not the case. There is a halo effect that has been placed over the founding fathers.

George Washington, the first US president, was a slaveholder throughout his life. He inherited slaves from his father and later acquired more through marriage and purchase. As I mentioned earlier in the book, Washington gave them one outfit of clothing per year, and he often made dentures for himself using teeth pulled from live enslaved people without the use of any anesthesia. It is a myth that his will allowed for the freedom of his slaves. They were inherited by his wife and later his descendants. He and his troops also engaged in various acts of violence and brutality against Indigenous peoples and their allies.

Thomas Jefferson owned hundreds of slaves throughout his life, and despite expressing ideas of freedom and equality in the Declaration of Independence, he never freed his own slaves during his lifetime. He fathered several children with Sally Hemings, the enslaved teenage half-sister of his wife. Hemings was not able to give her consent, so this was sexual abuse. As president, Jefferson signed the Indian Removal Act of 1830, which led to the forced relocation of thousands of Native Americans, known as the Trail of Tears, resulting in the deaths of thousands of Indigenous people.

Abraham Lincoln's initial position on slavery was one of gradual abolition rather than immediate abolition, and it was not until the middle of the Civil War that he issued the Emancipation Proclamation, which only freed slaves in the Confederate states, not the border states that remained loyal to the Union.

These men were all imperfect. Some were deeply flawed, but they were still able to profoundly impact the world.

This oversimplification and reduction of people to two-dimensional caricatures is not a uniquely American problem. History is written by the winners.

It's possible that good people opt out of leadership because they fear they do not meet a standard of perfection. By placing some on a pedestal, we deny them of their humanity and we cheat ourselves out of the opportunity to learn from them. Hellen Keller was a flawed person. Martin Luther King Jr. was a flawed person. Even Gandhi maintained a deeply racist belief in the caste system until his death. We cannot fear the truth of these stories. We can't learn from what we're afraid to look at.

Our temptation to protect the story must not outstrip our desire for the truth of the story. We cannot be selective in the lessons learned. Are we throwing away their accomplishments because of their wrongs? No. But we must learn from their errors. The genius of our founding fathers is they understood their fallibility and their humanity and gave us ways to create change as we changed. We have the opportunity and the duty to change as our access to information changes. In the words of Maya Angelou, "When you know better, you should do better."

You can say learning more about the behavior of these beloved characters doesn't change your opinion of them, but it is a mistake to hide their stories in an attempt to deny others the right to make that decision for themselves.

You don't have to be perfect to create a more perfect union.

TIME DOESN'T HEAL. HEALING HEALS.

In my work, there are a few core beliefs that emerge over and over again. One of the most enduring is, "You can't teach an old dog new tricks." This comment reassures us that things will change in the future. We just have to wait for the old generation of bigots to die off. Not only is this mean, but it's also not true.

There are definitely strides made by each generation, but those strides are achieved with work, not time. Time doesn't heal wounds. Healing heals wounds. We have to do the work of repair. How do I know this? Let's take a look at the ninth graders at Aledo High School.

Aledo is a high school twenty miles from Ft. Worth in North Texas. The district is affluent and overwhelmingly White. There are no Black teachers. Out of 499 ninth graders, 390 were White and only six were Black. In April 2021, the students created a Snapchat message titled "Slave Trade," and the six Black students were placed in the virtual slave auction.[53]

These children were reinventing what we have not had the courage to fully heal from. They had not grown out of it. They had actually modernized hate.

Now, just in case you are feeling smug and dismissive because this was a school in the South, please let me bring your attention to River Valley High School in California. In the fall of 2022, some members of the varsity football team posted a mock slave auction on social media. The Black members of the team were depicted standing in their underwear looking at the floor with nooses around their necks.[54]

Or the same year at Maugham Elementary School in Tenafly, New Jersey, where a fifth grader was asked to come to school dressed as her hero and she chose Adolf Hitler.[55]

There are more stories like this than I would care to list here. I share these not to shame the children, but to impress upon us adults that there is no substitute for doing the work. It is irresponsible leadership to punt the responsibility for improvement to the next generation. Leaders must lead.

Bigotry is uncanny in its ability to reinvent itself. We cannot hope to outgrow it; we must intentionally outperform it.

Chapter 8

Be a Placechanger

"What you do makes a difference, and you have to decide what kind of difference you want to make."

—JANE GOODALL

"**P**LEASE JOIN ME IN WELCOMING THE 2022 WORLD GOLF HALL OF Fame inductee, Tiger Woods!" The crowd leapt to their feet. In his speech, Tiger spoke about his work ethic. He talked about his parents' support of his love of the game. He thanked the leadership for agreeing to lower the qualifying age from fifty to forty-five for his induction, making him the youngest inductee in golf's history. I imagine that decision was not a hard one.

Tiger had a financial impact in the billions, but the "Tiger Woods effect" was not limited to just Tiger and the other top earners in the sport. His impact was felt by everyone. For example, in 1996, the season that Tiger Woods turned pro, the 125th-ranking person would earn approximately $167,000 dollars before expenses. For the 2021 season, the 125th-ranked player made $997,000. Before Tiger Woods, only ten golfers had ever grossed over $7 million. By 2017, more than 150 golfers had brought in over $10 million over the course of their careers.

Tiger brought an entirely new audience to the game. The viewership hours increased. The televised coverage of the sport increased, which created expanded revenue opportunities for every single stakeholder of the game. When Tiger played, everyone benefited, which makes it hard to believe that he almost didn't get to play.

When Tiger started playing on the junior circuit, he was denied access to some of the clubhouses of the country clubs where tournaments were played because of his race. While all the other players were inside getting dressed, he was forced to get dressed outside. One can hardly imagine what these acts of exclusion could have cost the game of golf.[56]

When you create the space and room to imagine and expand what's possible, you become a placechanger. Placechanging is critical. Whether you run a company, a family, or a Boy Scout troop, the willingness and commitment to changing spaces that historically excluded talented participants is the job of every leader. This work is often framed as charity or, even worse, a zero-sum game, the idea being, "I have to give something up in order to include you." But as Tiger's incredible example shows us, increasing opportunity expands the benefits for everyone. We need more placechangers.

In 1945, Gunder Hagg set a record of running a mile in 4:01. It was a commonly held belief that no human could run a mile in under four minutes. It was called "The Mount Everest of Athletic Achievement." There were even doctors who said it would be life-threatening. The record stood for nine years, until 1954 when Roger Bannister ran the mile in 3:59. This miracle didn't last long. The record stood for only forty-six days. Within two years, thirty-seven people had done it. On February 11, 2023, fifty-two runners ran under a four-minute mile in a single track meet.

Roger Bannister was a placechanger. As soon as people saw what was possible, they believed they could accomplish it as well. The utter debunking of what was thought to be an indisputable fact freed all runners to push the boundaries of their imagination. Placechanging has that effect.

When people see C-suite leaders like Ursula Burns or Sheryl Sandberg, not only can they celebrate them as individuals, but the change of place expands the idea of what a leader looks like. Not just as inspiration to the marginalized populations, but to the entire community as they get to see a reimagined picture of what a leader looks like, unlocking possibilities throughout the entire system.

We have many places that need to be changed. Too many places remain that leave talents like those of Tiger Woods out in the parking lot instead of in the clubhouse. Places like boardrooms, elite schools, segregated communities, and so many more. When we leave out women, minorities, the disabled, or those from lower socioeconomic backgrounds, we cheat ourselves out of the expanded opportunities that being Indivisible allows us. We cannot afford to waste genius. Indivisible leaders change the places that need to be changed so that no talent goes to waste.

SET THE TEMPO

Harold had been a manager for over twenty years. Throughout that time, his team had grown more and more diverse. The newest member, who was of South Asian descent, had a name that some found difficult to pronounce. One day Harold walked in on a conversation that gravely upset him. He overheard one of his floor supervisors say, "That name is just too hard. I'm gonna call you Sparky."

Harold intervened immediately, asking the new employee to simply state his name again clearly, then turned to the employees assembled and said, "It's my expectation that you will all take the time to learn to pronounce every person's name correctly. Write it down phonetically if you need to. In this organization, we respect people and take the time to pronounce their names correctly."

Harold is an incredible leader, and I'm sure it doesn't surprise you that he has an incredible track record of leadership within his organizations. But so often people will shorten names or assign some arbitrary nickname. They will say things like "That's a mouthful. I'll never remember that. I'm gonna call you X." This behavior is unacceptable from anyone, but the sheer amount of times it happens from leaders is disappointing.

This behavior leads many people to offer up an American version of their name, avoiding such disrespectful interactions altogether. It's an understandable choice and one we should respect if made. Others get angry. For them, each attempt to alter their name leads to a small confrontation of correction. This request for basic respect often results in the employee being labeled "difficult" and "combative."

If you can pronounce Siobhan and Tchaikovsky, you can make the effort to pronounce the names of coworkers correctly. It may seem like a small thing, but it's not. As leaders, we set the tone.

I've been fortunate to see this kind of bravery play out on an incredibly large scale. Leslie was the kind of leader they wrote articles about. She had started out as a waitress, and slowly, and incredibly worked her way up throughout the entire organization to become the leader. After running the company for several years, Leslie was eager to try a new challenge. She had no shortage of options. She was actively recruited by many other companies, because of her reputation for thoughtful, pragmatic decision-making, as well as her dynamic personality and leadership skills. She finally selected a company that had had some challenges, but also had an incredibly bright future. She knew she could make a difference there and eagerly started the new position as CEO.

As she always did when she started a new endeavor, she listened. She watched. She engaged the current employees to understand what was already happening to identify the areas that she would have to make changes to facilitate growth. The usual challenges reveal themselves in areas that were problematic, like communication, some leaders that had outlived their usefulness, some technology lags, and others. She had seen them all before. All but one.

The company had grown in the past ten years with a series of acquisitions, and as is often the case there had been challenges like supply chain issues, expansion struggles, and blending the cultures of the different acquisitions. But the most glaring? The women in the organization were being paid approximately ⅓ less than the men for the same positions. Leslie could not believe it. She gathered her leadership team to ask how this could happen.

They gave her an assortment of excuses. They explained how it had been unintentional, and how there was really no way to fix it at this point. They explained how they would do better in the future going forward. But Leslie is an Indivisible leader. Doing better in the future is not enough. When a wrong is identified, the harm is corrected.

Leslie immediately increased the salaries of the women who were being paid below scale.

This bold move is not without criticism. "It would be too expensive," said some. "She's going to bankrupt the company, " said others. "What will the people who didn't get raises say?" asked others. While all these concerns are important, none of them are more important than doing the right thing.

I tell you the story because of course it had a happy ending and we need to talk about happy endings way more than we do. Employee retention went through the roof and profitability increased. It turns out people want to work for an Indivisible leader. People want to work where they are treated fairly and where their leaders handle them honestly across difference, rather than disregard, or exploit those differences.

ARE FEELINGS FACTS?

One of the biggest challenges to change is managing the morale of the existing workforce. Too often, DEI has been presented as a boogeyman coming to steal your jobs. This isn't true, but as we've discussed earlier in this book, it doesn't have to be true to be deeply held. How do you persuade people who benefit from the status quo to welcome change instead of fearing and sabotaging it?

In an interview about his memoir with the *Sunday Times*, James Patterson, 75, lamented the perceived plight of White men in the entertainment industry, calling their struggle to find writing jobs in film, theater, TV, and publishing industries "just another form of racism."

"What's that all about? Can you get a job? Yes. Is it harder? Yes. It's even harder for older writers. You don't meet many 52-year-old White males."

James Patterson, the author of 318 published books that have collectively sold 425 million copies, was complaining that a White guy can't get a fair shot in the publishing industry. It was weird.

And he was 100 percent wrong. His rhetoric definitely does not match reality. A 2020 *New York Times* article stated 95 percent of American fiction books published between 1950 and 2018 were written by White people. 76 percent were written by men.[57]

The publishing industry, like many other industries, has a history of systemic racism and discrimination. The lack of diversity among authors, editors, and other publishing professionals has been well-documented, and studies have shown that books by and about people of color are often underrepresented and overlooked.

Additionally, publishing professionals from marginalized communities are underrepresented, with a majority of the industry being White and majority being women.

Furthermore, there are also reports that the publishing industry has a long history of gatekeeping, which is the process of preventing or limiting the success of marginalized groups in the industry. This includes the rejection of manuscripts written by authors of color, by those from marginalized communities, and the subsequent refusal to invest in the promotion and distribution of these books, making it harder for them to reach a wide readership.

I believe significant efforts are being made to change these practices. My hope is that the industry will broadly share these statistics as it improves. We need to celebrate success stories. What better place to find them than from the storytellers themselves?

In his defense, Patterson later apologized and withdrew his comments, saying, "I apologize for saying White male writers having trouble finding work is a form of racism. I absolutely do not believe that racism is practiced against White writers. Please know that I strongly support a diversity of voices being heard—in literature, in Hollywood, everywhere."[58]

We often say we acknowledge unfairness and that things need to change, but if we're honest, when that change actually comes, we sometimes process it through a lens of loss. It is important for us all to remember that every opportunity does not belong to you. Everyone has a right to participate in the systems and organizations that drive our culture. If there are people who have been excluded from those systems forever, we should welcome the opportunity to broaden their access, not complain that we are having to give up a small portion of the lion's share we have enjoyed heretofore. It's funny to me that people who are suddenly so concerned about fairness have never gone on the record to address the obvious disparities and underrepresentation of other groups.

We should use our positions of leadership and authority to create opportunities, not dampen them for others.

LOOK OUT FOR THE LITTLE GUY

During the pandemic lockdown, the world had the shared experience of commerce and social interactions shutting down. Workplaces and schools went dark as safety measures were implemented, and almost all of us were stuck at home, But even in the midst of this universally shared experience, we got a chance to see the many ways we are different.

I was participating in an all-team Zoom call for a financial services company. After the preliminary greetings and niceties, the managing director (MD) called the meeting to order. He noticed a few team members had their cameras off. He hated working remotely. He was a very hands-on manager and, prior to the lockdowns, he managed by walking around. He was trying to adjust to this new world, but he felt disconnected from his staff and was annoyed by those who refused to put their cameras on.

"Would everyone turn on their camera, please."

Most complied, but there was one holdout. Leah still had her camera off. The MD started to get angry. How disrespectful! People were really taking advantage of this situation. He hated to embarrass people, but he was not going to allow himself to be disrespected. It was his job to keep the cohesion of the team together even in these difficult circumstances. He had to make an example of this person. The team needed to understand that he was still in charge and there were still rules. If this person wanted a showdown, he would give it to them.

"Leah, please turn on your camera."

Leah turned on her camera and we all understood immediately why she hadn't. Leah had three children ages four, five, and eight, and they were bouncing off the walls. They seemed to be literally vibrating with cabin fever. Although Leah's sound was muted, the visuals of the kids pulling and jumping on her and the occasional projectile flying through the air were incredibly distracting.

The MD was more annoyed. Leah knew we were having this meeting. Why hadn't she figured out a way to entertain the kids so we could get through this important meeting? He forgot that this was one of five Zoom meetings that were happening this way for her today alone.

"Leah, it's a little distracting where you are. Could you move to another room?"

She answered without missing a beat: "I don't have another room."

Everyone on the call froze. The MD had made a tragic mistake. His quarantine experience was stressful, but it was comfortable. When news of the lockdown came, he and his family decided to ride it out at his 5,000-square-foot lake house. As he sat on this call, he was sitting in his private office overlooking the lake while his stay-at-home wife was downstairs taking care of his kids. He didn't even have to hear them, let alone entertain them or manage their remote school experience.

Leah on the other hand, lived in a 950-square-foot apartment. She had always been a fantastic contributor. She was a creative problem-solver who had stitched together a network of resources and systems to make her life as a single mom work on her modest salary. With the lockdown in place, every one of those support networks had vanished in the blink of an eye.

She has sacrificed space to be in a good school district, because unfortunately, the schools in the neighborhoods she could more easily afford were terrible. The tight space hadn't really bothered her before, because the kids were at school and aftercare most of the day, and as a family, they spent a great deal of time outside of the house running errands and doing activities. The pandemic changed everything. Now they rarely left the house, and the walls were closing in on them.

Her mother would help with child care and support, but she was in the most at-risk population and was in delicate health. Consequently, she could not see the kids at all. That meant it was all Leah all the time taking care of three kids, their schoolwork, and her full-time job.

So she didn't have another room. She couldn't make this any better. She was doing the best she could. And the MD had embarrassed her in front of everyone.

He was mortified. He didn't know all the details of her life. But the truth of it is, he had made a mistake that many of us make. We assume we are all experiencing life in the same way.

Even if we are all fighting the same battle, we are not always doing it with the same tools and under the same conditions.

The Bureau of Labor Statistics reported that in 2020, around 76.5 percent of single mothers were in the labor force.[59] As a society, we need them to be able to provide for their children. We need to create pathways to success for them wherever possible. We don't want unnecessary practices that cheat us out of the contributions they are capable of making to our organizations. I often see companies wax philosophically about how much they care about family values. That's wonderful to put in a brochure, but where does that manifest in your processes? Do parents get the opportunity to thrive there? Is there flexibility when possible? Are people penalized for having lives?

All employees are not the same and not everyone will be affected by policies in the same way. This is where exploring edge cases becomes essential. An edge case is a scenario that falls outside of the norm and may require special consideration. For example, an employee with a disability may require accommodations that are not provided for in a typical policy. If this edge case is not explored, the employee may not be able to fully participate in the workplace, which can lead to decreased productivity and morale.

Exploring edge cases also allows for greater inclusivity and diversity within the workplace. By considering the needs of a diverse group of employees, policies can be created that are more inclusive and equitable. This can lead to a more positive and productive work environment for all employees.

Exploring edge cases is crucial when developing human resources policies. It allows for the needs of all employees to be considered, which can lead to a more inclusive and productive work environment.

The environment we create for our employees matters. Concert violinist Joshua Bell proved this point when he conducted an experiment in 2007. He went into a Washington, DC, Metro subway station and put out a hat for donations. He then went on to play his Stradivarius violin for forty-five minutes. This premier musician, who earns about $15 million a year, made just $32.17.[60] His playing was superb, but the conditions weren't right for his talent to be appropriately appreciated.

As leaders, are we creating the right environment for our employees to shine? Are we creating the space? Each person has unique talents that require thoughtfulness and intentionality to harness. Everyone is not the same. If a fish and a scuba diver meet in the ocean, they may appear the same. They're both in the water. They're both breathing. They're both moving. But let the air run out of the scuba diver's tank and you will quickly see how different they are.

There are members of your team who have different sets of variables that impact the amount of effort required for them to thrive. A recent immigrant for whom English is a second language has a different experience than a US-born father with a stay-at-home wife. Both have gifts worthy of development. Both can contribute wildly to your team. Some people expend more energy to get the same result. We need to understand that. And devise strategies to develop each one.

Chapter 9

Ask for Help

"Closed mouths don't get fed."

—SOUTHERN PROVERB

JENNIFER HAD BEEN A PARENT AT A PRIVATE SCHOOL FOR FOUR years. She was an active volunteer who cared deeply about the quality of the education and the community her children experienced at the school.

Part of how that community is created is by a high level of parent involvement. To foster that involvement, the school was hosting a parent committee drive where different committees would introduce themselves so parents could select their committee service for the year.

Jennifer was head of the gardening committee. The school was fortunate to have a beautiful spacious campus where crops could be raised, and Jennifer was excited to cultivate some new plants. You see Jennifer had been deeply touched by the murder of George Floyd. Like so many others, she had read many books and attended many trainings urging her to do something in her own life to address the ignorance that perpetuates racism. As an Asian woman, she empathized with the minority experience and wanted to do some small part to help.

Each committee head introduced their plan in front of the crowded, bustling room of parents, until finally it was Jennifer's turn. She talked about the history of the garden and the hours of service, but what she said next stopped everyone in their tracks.

"This year, in an effort to better understand and respect the African American experience of slavery, we will be growing and harvesting cotton."

You could have heard a pin drop. The parent reactions ranged from outrage to discomfort. But no one was more uncomfortable than Jennifer. What she had meant as a practical tactile experience of a little-understood period of our history had become a powder keg of frustration and anger.

I applaud Jennifer's desire to be helpful. I believe her intention was pure. In a time when we are telling people to do what they can where they can, she legitimately thought this was an excellent teaching moment. She was using an activity within her control to expand understanding.

But here's where she went wrong: She didn't use her resources. The school had a director of diversity, equity, and inclusion. It also had a Black Parents Association. Either of these would have been excellent sources for Jennifer to seek feedback from.

It's OK—even important—to be creative, but you should couple that with humility and draw up your resources, especially when addressing sensitive issues.

Just because you have an idea, does not mean:
- It is time for that idea.
- This is the right context for that idea.
- You are the right person to execute that idea.
- The idea has been communicated effectively.

Had she consulted others, Jennifer might have realized that making such an incendiary statement to a crowded, distracted group of fidgety parents was less than ideal, maybe a well-crafted email or letter home would have been more appropriate. She might have understood the value of having a Black parent make the suggestion with her to show that she had taken the time to consider their feelings. She also might have realized that the constant reminder of enslaved people picking cotton would have exposed the number of Black students to cruel teasing at the hands of immature middle schoolers and was not a good idea at all.

There could have been so much learning if only she had asked.

I don't believe in eating Allies. I also don't believe that every well-intentioned idea is a good one. There are wild opportunities somewhere in between.

You may remember the game show *Who Wants to Be a Millionaire?* where contestants answered a series of trivia questions that, if they got all correct, would win them $1 million. One of the tools you could use if you got stuck was "Phone a Friend," which allowed you to call a preselected friend and ask them to help you choose the right multiple-choice answer.

The premise is two minds are better than one. I was always fascinated by this part of the show because of the beautiful simplicity of it. The contestant needed both the humility to say "I don't know," and a profound trust in whom they asked. This is true for all of us.

Have you built humility and trust into your lives and processes? Are you afraid to ask? Epictetus said, "It is impossible for a man to learn what he thinks he already knows." All improvement comes from a place of humility. Curiosity is the way to wisdom and it starts with the courage to ask for help.

WHAT ASKING GETS YOU

You need someone to help you see the problem and have the humility to ask them. It is not enough to do your best; you must know what to do, and then do your best. How do you know what you have to do? You ask.

Let's say you're a business leader wanting to make a major change in a human resources policy. You could unilaterally review the data to make a decision about the right way forward. Alternatively, you could assemble a small focus group representative of the different demographic groups that make up your workforce and ask them.

Imagine the rich information you would get from this process. You might learn the frustrations single employees have with the expectation

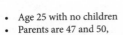

- Only child of a single mom
- No other family in the area
- Travels the country to run marathons

- Age 25 with no children
- Parents are 47 and 50, and in great health
- Frustrated by how often he's asked to stay late because other employees have "families"

Solution

- Has three sisters, two are stay-at-home moms
- Has a stay-at-home wife
- Parents are currently in a nursing home

- Asian
- Currently caring for two parents in their 80s
- Culturally unacceptable to put parents in a nursing home

that they will work every holiday or every late-night project. You might learn that additional managerial training is needed based on how culturally different groups think about elder care. Maybe your current policies allow for care for a sick child, but your managers may be resistant to employees taking time off to care for a sick parent. This process also might reveal the different PTO needs employees have based on their family structure. Larger families are going to have more incidents of illness that require time off. People with smaller families may not have anyone to share the responsibility of caretaking with. How should these issues shape your decision-making? The value of this additional information is invaluable to creating the best possible policy.

Can you make every decision by committee? Of course not. But when possible, this can be an invaluable tool. There is an old saying: "No talking about us, without us." When you include the impacted populations in the decision-making that affects them, you're going to learn things you weren't aware of. You tap into a treasure trove of valuable insight that makes everyone more satisfied. There is a not-so-subtle disrespect in excluding people. Whenever possible, ask.

Life is better and you are much smarter when your sentences have more question marks than periods. It is tempting to want to always be the expert, but we have to get more comfortable being the student. We need to ask more questions. It can be more time consuming, more laborious, even more expensive, but it's worth it.

SPREAD THE LOVE AND THE WORK

> *"Talent wins games, but teamwork and intelligence win championships."*
>
> —MICHAEL JORDAN

Cindy and Harris were burned out. Fried actually. They were two members of a nineteen-member leadership team for a midsize corporation. In the wake of the brutal murder of George Floyd at the hands of police, the company had adopted several new DEI initiatives. One of these efforts was the creation of seven affinity groups or employee resource groups (ERGs) such as the Black Employees Alliance, the Women's Network, and the Pride Network.

The purpose of these groups was to:
- Provide peers with a safe space, enhance employee well-being, and foster a more inclusive workplace.
- Provide insights and perspectives that may not be represented elsewhere within the organization.
- Help organizations build a robust pipeline of underrepresented talent and help ensure these employees don't leave within the first two years of employment, as sometimes happens.
- Create a safe, supportive space for employees who share a common aspect of identity.
- Strengthen the work environment by providing employees with webinars, mentorship, and other programs to enhance their growth and satisfaction.

Each group required an executive sponsor to be associated with it. The role of that executive sponsor was to:

- **Shepherd:** Help navigate the organization's systems and bureaucracy.
- **Supervise:** Act as a sounding board and advisor for activities of the group to ensure they are aligned with the values and business goals of the company.
- **Support:** Encourage the leaders and members of the ERGs.

Cindy and Harris were eager to participate in these initiatives. They wanted to be a vital part of this dimension of the future growth of the company. Their CEO had shared his vision for a more inclusive organization, and they were excited to help bring that vision to reality.

It went well for a while. At first they were each sponsoring one or two groups and that was manageable, but as new groups came online, none of the other executives on the leadership team were willing to step up to be sponsors. Not wanting to see the effort stall, Cindy and Harris each took on the responsibility of more groups.

And they were fried.

I was brought in as a consultant to this company. In a meeting with the CEO, he proudly asked my opinion about the ERG program that the company had initiated. One of the challenging parts of my role as an inclusion strategist is answering questions like this when I know the client is proud of their efforts and I have to bust their bubble.

"On a scale of one to ten, I give it a two," I said. He almost spit out the water he was drinking, "A two?" He couldn't believe my answer.

"Tom, there are a number of reasons someone starts an ERG program. Sometimes it's to catalyze belonging and the development of leadership skills within different populations in the company. Sometimes it's because of employee demand. Sometimes it's just a public relations move to respond to board pressure and satisfy external critics. Why did you create the ERG program?"

"We did it to show our commitment to the value of diversity and to support our employees."

"Do you think you're doing that?"

"Absolutely," he said.

And he did believe that. Like so many leaders, he thought setting up a well-intentioned program was enough. But here's what he did not see.

The fact that only two members of the leadership team sponsored all seven ERGs had not gone unnoticed. On the contrary, it was openly ridiculed by the ERG leadership and its members. The common feeling was that Cindy and Harris supported these goals, not the company. The efforts were individualized instead of advancing company culture.

The only two executive leaders willing to do the work were from underrepresented groups themselves. Cindy was a woman and Harris was LGBTQ. The terrible message sent was "Actually, the company doesn't care about this. These groups will have to fend for themselves. Only marginalized people can drive change (even though the problem is largely not theirs). This is a small-group problem, not a company-wide need."

The absence of other leader involvement underscored that DEI was not actually a strongly held value in the company, reinforcing the concerns and complaints of underrepresented employees.

Because Cindy and Harris were doing all the work, they were exhausted and were quickly becoming resentful of the other leaders. What started as a shared value was quickly becoming a wedge between them.

Cindy and Harris were doing this work on top of all their other duties. No space or accommodation was made for these additional tasks. Essentially, their peers had more time to do less work. Cindy and Harris were effectively being penalized for helping advance a company goal.

The perception is that the CEO doesn't care. Why? Because the leaders will do what the CEO deems important. The fact that Tom hadn't even noticed this glaring problem telegraphs to the leadership and the whole company that this doesn't matter. If it doesn't matter to Tom, it doesn't matter to anyone.

Tom is not unique. Many leaders falter when it comes to consistently sharing the work and the rewards of creating Indivisible teams. They try to delegate the responsibility for this important cultural change to human resources or a DEI lead (often with small, underfunded teams), but these efforts are marginally successful.

You cannot outsource culture creation. A true leader takes responsibility and ownership for culture changes. If an organization is going to be truly Indivisible, the work and the reward must include everyone, everywhere, every day.

ALL HANDS ON DECK

As we saw with Cindy and Harris, this work is a lot less fun when it is not shared. One group that I have seen be disproportionately utilized are Black and Brown employees and women in the company recruiting process.

Companies everywhere have turned their attention to recruiting from these critical employee groups. Very often, current employees are asked to assist with these recruiting efforts. Have worked with clients that had one Black person and one woman on their large teams and asked that those employees attend EVERY interview with a diverse candidate. This additional responsibility is often not compensated additionally beyond salary and the duties of that employee's original position are not adjusted in any way. The cumulative effect is that the employees who are underrepresented themselves and managing their own journey through a predominantly White male environment, now have the additional burden of recruiting new employees which is not their job. They do this with an expectation of excellent performance in their role with added scrutiny of being othered in their environment. They are not superheroes or martyrs. They are not representative of their group and while they can and should play a part in cultural change, too often they are expected to be the owners of it.

A challenge I often see is when training and skills development is only provided in one segment of the business. The front line gets training the executives are not required to attend or the reverse. The executives do deep-dive training and retreats, but the employees get minimal exposure to the information. Cultural value transmission must happen at every level of the organization for it to have a chance of happening.

Part 3

MOVE FROM THE MIDDLE

Chapter 10

Swap the Nouns

"We do not see things as they are, we see things as we are."

—ANAÏS NIN

ONE OF THE MOST SUCCESSFUL DEVICES I USE IN MY BUSINESS IS to swap the nouns. Whenever you are unclear about how to think about or handle a situation. Swap the nouns. Let's take our pregnant belly touchers. They say they do it for good luck. Well, I've heard it is good luck to rub a bald man's head, especially if it is shaved clean. Isn't it funny that you never hear of people walking up to their boss and rubbing his bald head for luck? I wonder why. My guess is we respect the boss and respect the boundary of his personal space. What if we sought to respect everyone in the same way? You don't need a checklist, you need a process. Are there behaviors you practice or tolerate for others that you wouldn't do in other situations? Ask yourself why.

One night I went down the rabbit hole on YouTube and came across a video of a social experiment. Men are gathered to watch a video of a woman walking down the street being catcalled. Largely, they feel like the behavior is harmless, even funny. Then the woman is substituted by their wife, girlfriend, or sister. All of a sudden, their assessment of the catcalling behavior shifts. Now it is disrespectful, unacceptable, and angering. In this experiment, all they did was swap the nouns.

Could a security guard follow your daughter around the store without you being upset? Could the men in the meeting cut your wife off or steal her ideas and pass them off as their own? Could your son's coworkers change his name because they didn't want to take the time to learn to pronounce it?

When in doubt, swap the nouns. Try to think of a situation or person you care about and rewrite the scenario so you can assess your consistency and make sure you are not centering yourself in your evaluation.

THE ART OF MAKING SPACE

Robert manages an engineering firm in Oklahoma. His work requires him and his team to travel to various client worksites many times throughout the day. Trust that the work is being done is required between him, as the manager, and his team members.

One December day, Robert returned to the office between meetings to find Muhammed, one of his employees, sitting in his car in the parking garage with his eyes closed. It appeared that Muhammed was sleeping. Robert angrily approached him, disappointed that his top performer would be so unprofessional. When he reached the car, he was surprised to see that Muhammed actually had his eyes closed, holding a prayer rug.

Robert knocked on the window and asked him why he was sitting in the cold garage. Muhammed said one of the tenets of his faith is to pray several times a day. He knows some people in the office are suspicious of Muslims, so he decided to come out to the car so he wouldn't make anyone uncomfortable. "As the only non-Christian employee, I don't want to stick out any more than I already do."

Robert said OK and continued on into the office. As he entered the building lobby, he became more sensitive to the Christmas decorations everywhere. He saw the same in his office. For the first time, he noticed how his religion was accommodated to the exclusion of all others.

When Muhammed came into the office, Robert took him to an empty office and said "This is your dedicated space to pray. I never want you to feel like you have to go to your car again. If we can make space for a Christmas tree for a month, we can make space for you to pray for a few minutes during the day."

Being sensitive and respectful of the religious beliefs of others is powerful because it can be so central to their identity. While no one can be expected to be an expert in every religion, it is deeply respectful to take the time to make an effort to learn about such an important pillar in people's lives.

Some people get overwhelmed with this idea. They say things like "We can't accommodate EVERYBODY." My response to that is "Yes you can." I have clients who structure the company schedules around the start of hunting season because so many members of the industry are active hunters. If we can accommodate the shooting of animals for fun, I'm sure we can accommodate someone's religious observance. When we care about people, we make space for what's important to them.

THE HELPLESS EXPERT

He said they just couldn't figure it out.

In a June 2020 memo to employees, Charles W. Scharf, who became the chief executive of Wells Fargo the year before, pledged to consider a wider array of candidates for jobs at the bank, but added that the bank struggled to find qualified Black candidates.[61]

"The unfortunate reality is that there is a very limited pool of Black talent to recruit from with this specific experience," he said.

This statement strikes me as odd. Wells Fargo is one of the country's largest banks. It has been around since 1852. They are the ones who provide the specific experience to do their work. They literally could have raised their own leaders. Instead, they give excuses.

This seems like a strange position for a trusted advisor to take. As a large bank, Wells Fargo purports to help clients manage and make wise decisions about their assets. How can that be true if the bank cannot even address its own challenges? Especially when they have more tools than most to do so?

His comments triggered backlash, and he later apologized for the comment when the memo became public in September. I don't know about you, but I don't want excuses from my advisors. I want results.

What makes this situation even worse is that Wells Fargo/Wachovia got its start on the backs of slavery. They are not alone. Aetna, AIG, JP Morgan Chase, Tiffany & Co, New York Life, and many other prestigious institutions profited directly from the buying and selling of Black bodies.[62] They profited from racial disparity, but they can't figure out how to address racial disparity today.

I wish I could say that this legacy of bad behavior was ancient history, but that wouldn't be true. Wells Fargo has settled several discrimination cases in recent years. In 2012, the company agreed to pay more than $175 million to settle allegations from the Justice Department that it steered Black and Latino borrowers into expensive loans and charged them excessive fees. As part of the settlement, Wells Fargo did not admit wrongdoing, saying it treated all of its customers fairly but wanted to avoid protracted litigation.

A lawsuit filed in a San Francisco federal court in 2022 argues that Wells Fargo's practices push Black homeowners into foreclosure, which *Bloomberg* referred to as a modern form of redlining. Wells Fargo is the largest bank mortgage lender in the country, but it accepted less than half of Black mortgage refinancing applicants in 2020. Seventy-two percent of White refinancing applicants were approved, compared to just 47 percent of Black applicants.

In 2020, the bank, which has more than 260,000 employees, settled allegations by the Labor Department that it discriminated against more than 34,000 Black and more than 300 female applicants by conducting "fake interviews" of diverse candidates for positions that were already filled, in a bid to boost diversity efforts on paper. Clearly the bank was able to get creative in solving some problems, just not the problem of inclusion.

In the settlement, Wells Fargo agreed to pay $7.8 million in back wages and interest to 580 affected applicants and to provide these people with job opportunities as tellers, personal bankers, customer sales and service representatives, and other positions. The settlement did not require Wells Fargo to admit liability but, in addition to taking the remedial steps just described, the bank was required to allow federal officials to proactively monitor some of its business operations and compliance measures.

What if we, as leaders and professionals, took responsibility for the results our organizations were delivering instead of acting as the helpless expert? In what ways are you making excuses for inequitable situations around you?

Let's stop apologizing for unacceptable situations. Indivisible leaders take responsibility. They direct their considerable strength and power toward solutions. They resolve situations, not excuse them.

YOU ARE NOT THE STAR OF EVERY STORY

One of the biggest challenges to being Indivisible is the very human habit of putting ourselves at the center of every story. Looking at things exclusively from our perspective.

My friend Abdul has been blind for over half his life. He had been on the waiting list for a service animal for quite some time and was so excited when he finally got Lucky. Lucky was a loving, gentle golden retriever who changed Abdul's life overnight. The freedom, independence, and mobility allowed Abdul to experience so many different things. After a lifetime of requiring an escort, he could go shopping by himself. He could go to the park by himself. On one occasion, Lucky prevented Abdul from stepping off of a train platform. The link between them was transformative. As he got to know Lucky, he also learned more about people. Because Lucky is such a beautiful dog, people often wanted to pet or play with him. Now, if you know anything about service dogs, you know you're not supposed to touch them because they are working. There was one incident where Lucky was distracted and Abdul walked into a steel pole, requiring four stitches. Because so many people violated this boundary, Abdul had a sign made that hung from Lucky's neck that said "Please don't touch me. I'm working."

One day a woman and her toddler approached Lucky and started playing with him. Abdul felt for the sign, thinking he may have forgotten to attach it, but it was clearly there, so he was forced to ask the woman for her and her child to stop playing with the dog. Surprisingly, the woman immediately became hostile. "What's the big deal? My son just wants to play with your dog. He's not hurting anything." Abdul replied "It's dangerous for me because I need him to be focused. If he's distracted, I could get hurt."

But the woman didn't care. She ignored him and her son continued to play with the dog. In doing so, she revealed a source of conflict that is often unacknowledged. She didn't want her child to cry. That would've been uncomfortable for her. So, she selfishly prioritized her comfort over Abdul's need for safety. This happens more often than you think. A woman brought her sick child into an urgent care clinic. She wanted him to see a doctor, but was upset by the fact that all the doctors in the clinic were immigrants from various Asian countries. She demanded to see a White doctor. When asked why, she said, "I would just be more comfortable." This need for comfort is a thread through many negative interactions across difference.

We are in a culture that values comfort over much else. Buddhists call it "the Precious Me." The idea is that all beings have a natural inclination toward self-centeredness and self-preservation, but through spiritual practice and cultivation of wisdom, one can learn to transcend this narrow perspective and develop a more compassionate and selfless outlook.

One of the key practices in Buddhism to overcome self-centeredness is the cultivation of empathy and compassion. This is done by developing an understanding of the interconnectedness of all beings, recognizing that all beings are subject to suffering and that we all share a common humanity.

We have to learn to accommodate the needs of others.

All too often, we center ourselves. We place our comfort, pleasure, and convenience above those of others.

I am often asked to give people a checklist of what to do and what not to do when it comes to bridging difference. What words they should avoid and where do most sensitive points of conflict occur? I wish there was some big list I could give them, but there isn't. My list has one action on it: Understand that you are not the star of every story.

A perfect example of this is the habit of touching Black women's hair. This is a strange point of contention, but one that comes up often in my work. Some Black women tend to change their hairstyles often and sometimes the styles are very different than what is possible for other races due to the texture. Any time there is a difference, it will invite curiosity. That's perfectly fine, but what often happens is people will reach out and touch that woman's (and sometimes man's) hair without their permission. This can be extremely uncomfortable and upsetting for the Black person because it violates their personal space.

As people learn about this discomfort, some are really surprised that anyone would take offense. They think it is a harmless gesture. I have had the hair touchers explain that they "didn't mean any harm" and they "don't see the big deal." As if their understanding is required for them to respect someone else's boundaries.

I've consulted on a few cases where the same thing happens to pregnant women. People think rubbing the pregnant woman's stomach will give them good luck, so they reach out and rub her baby bump without consent. I want you to imagine any other scenario where a coworker could come up to you and rub their hands over your stomach without your permission. It would be unacceptable. We tend to understand boundaries for ourselves, but we don't always honor those boundaries for others.

As an inclusion strategist, I am often privy to the concerns of different populations in the workplace. One group I think we don't talk enough about is single, childless workers. I have seen truly disrespectful interactions between the rest of the team toward childless employees. They are often expected to work holidays because "they don't have a family" as if they aren't someone's son or daughter. They are often asked to pick up the slack for parents who are dealing with sick children or just coaching the little league game. I've seen people receive significant pressure to cancel any plans they may have because of the needs of people with children. The suggestion that the lives of people who don't have children are empty or not as demanding or worthy of respite as yours is unfair.

Once again, you are not the star of every story. It is important to be respectful of everyone.

FLYOVER STATE

A friend of mine had a New York City–based startup that was doing really well. She was fundraising, and since her product had particular applications in places like Texas, where I live, she asked if I would share her deck with investors and high-net-worth individuals I knew in my area. I happily agreed to help, since I know firsthand the challenges women face fundraising and I loved her idea.

When I got the deck, I reviewed it. (You should never share a deck you haven't looked at yourself). In it, she laid out her approach. Imagine my surprise when I got to the slide explaining her marketing strategy as targeting "flyover states."

A flyover state is a term for all the insignificant places you "fly over" to get to the important places like New York and LA. I grew up in New York, and I have lived in LA. I know there can be a snobbish disdain for people who don't live in those cities, but I was shocked to see it printed and normalized in a pitch deck.

I called her immediately and shared my concerns and, of course, she removed it. But the idea that you would ask people for money while simultaneously disrespecting and dismissing them was jarring. Everyone loves their home. Even New York and LA are not the centers of the universe.

We must move from the middle.

iﬁcant pressure to c
ﬁds of people
ﬁon

Chapter 11

Get Creative

*"Understand that the right to choose your own path is
a sacred privilege. Use it. Dwell in possibility."*

—OPRAH WINFREY

"**I** WAS REALLY EXCITED ABOUT HIS PROMOTION, BUT I'M AFRAID I'M
going to have to quit."

James was a front-line technician and his incredible work ethic and
technical skill earned him a new role that required him to travel to a
job site in another city five days a week to complete a two-month project. This was an exciting evolution for James' career and he excitedly
jumped into his new role.

Then he hit a massive problem. The company required employees
to pay for their own travel and get reimbursed a few weeks later. For
middle-class and upper-class employees with credit cards, this was no
problem. For employees like James, this was a disaster. James had experienced a medical bankruptcy a few years before due to the expense of
caring for his sick son, so he lived a cash existence with no credit cards.

For his job, he had to buy plane tickets and pay for multiple nights
in a hotel. He also had to pay for a rental car, gas, and food for weeks at
a time. He had received a raise with his new position and he knew he
would be reimbursed for these expenses eventually, but in the meantime, he couldn't afford to pay his rent. While he was away from his
family, he lived on one-dollar burritos from the gas station so his fam-

ily didn't go without. The longer the project went on, the worse the situation got. James literally could not afford to work.

He went to his manager Rick to resign, and Rick was shocked. This is an issue that had never occurred to anyone in leadership before. James had the skills and the will to do the work. He just didn't have the financial positioning necessary to conduct his work. The company policies had inadvertently created a caste of jobs that were out of the reach of some people no matter how talented they were.

Rick sprang into action. He booked major travel for James for the next few weeks on his company card. He also expedited the pending reimbursement expenses owed to James and arranged a small cash advance that allowed James to conduct his work without worry for his family.

More importantly, Rick brought the issue to the leadership team which catalyzed an in-depth process review. No one wanted to lose great employees because they were struggling financially. They, with great care and respect, interviewed other employees to ensure this issue wasn't happening to them as well. They then created an alternate path for expense management for all employees going forward. In an Indivisible organization, they understand that everyone one's experience is different, but we tend to create policies for people like us. Only when we decenter ourselves and our experience can we truly have a place where everyone can thrive.

Experts fail because they're experts in a world that no longer exists. The world is ever-changing and we must change with it. That requires humility and a deep acceptance that our experience is not the only experience that matters.

I saw this a lot during the debate over the government's plan to forgive student loan debt for people who were low income. I heard countless people complain that, forty years ago, they had worked summers during high school to save for college or that they worked two jobs flipping burgers and babysitting to pay college expenses. They felt it was unfair to forgive the debt. Why couldn't today's young people do the same? But they left out a few details.

In 1973, the average four-year degree was $503. There were a number of state colleges that were entirely free. In 2021, the average cost of a four-year degree was $102,828.[63] I'm pretty sure there aren't enough burgers in the world to cover that bill. People were centering the argument based on their own past experience without taking the time to understand the realities of the present day.

We have to allow for the changing landscape of experience and resist the temptation to interact with outdated perspectives and information. This requires deep listening and humility. Things change, and we have to be ready to change with them.

MORE THAN ONE WAY TO SKIN A CAT

Our old, half-blind diabetic dog Tiger was the sweetest dog you would ever meet. He was a little dachshund that would shower you with kisses at every opportunity. Contrast that with the beast that lived next door. The 100-pound dog was the most aggressive I'd ever encountered in my life. Every time we came into our backyard, he would bark and hurl his body violently at the fence.

Tiger would never bark back and would only be in the backyard if one of us was there. It turns out, our little dog was prophetic.

One day, I was coming out of the house into the backyard when I passed Tiger flying into the house in terror. The fence had finally surrendered to the force of the neighbor's dog. It was down, and the neighbor's dog was now aggressively entering our backyard.

Like Tiger, I turned to run back into the house. You can imagine my surprise when my husband ran the other way. He actually ran toward the dog. He grabbed his snout and laid his weight across him to restrain him. I was stunned. And horrified. Never in a million years did I think he would do that. As the dog struggled and scratched at my husband, my daughter ran to get the neighbor to retrieve his dog.

My heroic husband was sweaty and blood ran down his arm from some of the many scratches he had received. I believe he saved lives that day, but I was furious at the risk he had taken, and I was clear I would not have taken that risk. I did not feel equipped to physically restrain an angry dog.

Sometimes, when we ask people to courageously intervene when they see racist, sexist, or otherwise inappropriate behavior, they are afraid. They think we are asking them to metaphorically restrain an angry, ferocious dog.

But there are always multiple ways to help. My husband took the most aggressive (and most dangerous) way but there were several other choices he could have made. He could have banged on the neighbor's door to alert him of the situation. He could have grabbed a stick and scared the dog away. He could have called 911 or warned other neighbors that the dog was free. All of those choices would have been helpful to the situation.

There is a continuum of involvement. You don't have to do everything, but you can't do nothing. There is a continuum of bystander behavior. The minimum is witness. I often think about Darnella Frazier, the seventeen-year-old who filmed the brutal murder of George Floyd. Her simple act of filming the crime on her cell phone changed the world.

There are always options, but the only unacceptable option is to do nothing.

The Most
Extreme Option

Restrain a
ferocious dog

Other Possible
Options

Bang on dog
owner's door

Call 911

Scare dog off

Warn all the neighbors

Each one of us is capable of creatively generating ways to help if we don't look away and make excuses.

I was afraid that day and fear can sometimes dampen our creativity and our ability to respond. I understand that sometimes you might be afraid to speak up or challenge authority. But when you don't, you become part of the problem. If everyone just looks away, the behavior will never change.

So I challenge you to get creative. Let's say a coworker expresses a racist comment in a gathering of you and other coworkers.

You could:

- Confront them in front of everyone, right on the spot.
- Make a comment at the end of the meeting about the inappropriateness of the comment.
- Ask them to explain what they meant by the comment.
- Leave the meeting in protest.
- Pull them to the side after the meeting.
- Report the comment to your supervisor or HR.

What if you're in a store and you see another customer being harassed and racially profiled?

You could:

- Tell the store employee to stop.
- Ask the victim of the profiling if they need help.

- Record the incident.
- Call the police.
- Stand in close proximity to the victim.
- Share your account of the situation with others after the incident to change policy.

All of these options vary in risk. I understand that sometimes we feel like we do not have the power or the position to select the most aggressive or confrontational solution, but that shouldn't mean we do nothing.

It's often tempting to sit in the helplessness of the situation instead of being proactive about how we change it. You are never helpless. There is always some action you can take, if you look for it. How do we make it wildly different? How do we get creative? Innovative? How do we challenge ourselves to look for ways to create a shift?

BE OPEN TO RIDICULOUS SOLUTIONS

Albert Einstein famously said, "If at first an idea is not absurd, then there is no hope for it."

Now, I have a caution for you. There are times when this process will call for imperfect solutions. There is no ten-second solution for a ten-generation problem. We will have insufficient remedies. There will be some who think the policies and changes made will be unrealistic in the "real world." I challenge you to have the courage to embrace imperfect solutions. To move forward.

The Three-Fifths Compromise came about as a way to resolve the disagreement between Northern and Southern states over the issue of representation in the United States House of Representatives. The Northern states wanted representation to be based on the free population, while the Southern states wanted representation to be based on the number of free citizens plus their large populations of enslaved people. Southern states argued that the enslaved were a significant economic asset and should be represented in Congress, while Northern states opposed counting enslaved people as full persons for the purposes of representation, as they did not have the same rights as free persons and were not considered citizens.

During the Constitutional Convention of 1787, a committee was formed to address the issue, which eventually proposed the compromise that, for the purpose of apportioning representatives and direct taxes, each slave would be counted as three-fifths of a person. This compromise helped to break the deadlock, allowing the convention to move forward with drafting the United States Constitution, and was ultimately included in Article I, Section 2, Clause 3 of the United States Constitution.

This idea was preposterous. It was ridiculous. It was a political agreement that did not change the status of enslaved people as property, but instead only counted them as fractional persons for the purpose of increasing slaveholding states' representation in Congress. But it was the way forward and, as wild as it was, it got us here.

We're still making these kinds of compromises today. Take the EMERGE Program in Houston, Texas. This incredible program operates in public high schools to help low-income, first-generation students gain admission to elite schools all over the country. They have placed over 1,500 students at schools like MIT, Harvard, Yale, Stanford, and many more. Their success has been incredible, but it in no way mitigates our responsibility as a nation to provide equitable access to educational opportunities for all students, regardless of their economic standing. It is an insufficient solution that only serves a small portion of the 15.3 million high school students in America. The root problem has not been solved. Our schools should equip everyone. In a perfect world, a program like EMERGE wouldn't be necessary. In the meantime, I'm glad programs like EMERGE level the playing field.

We have to stay open to solutions we can build on. Solutions that move things forward.

DISAGREE WITHOUT DESTRUCTION

The Fairness Doctrine was a policy enforced by the Federal Communications Commission (FCC) in the United States from 1949 to 1987.

It required that holders of broadcast licenses (such as radio and television stations) present controversial issues of public importance in a balanced and impartial manner. The doctrine was intended to ensure that the public was exposed to diverse viewpoints on controversial issues, but it was repealed by the FCC in 1987.

By requiring broadcast stations to provide balanced coverage of controversial issues, the Fairness Doctrine made it difficult and expensive for those stations to air controversial or one-sided programming. This created an opening for alternative forms of media, such as cable news channels, which were not subject to the same regulations.

Unfortunately, these networks have become a training model for destructive disagreement. Asserting every day that people who disagree with you are morons, fascists, Nazis, or Communists. These examples have seeped into our broader cultural conversation. As Indivisible leaders, we must be careful not to adopt this good/bad, heaven/hell simplistic reductionist thinking. We must seek out nuance and we must process our disagreements in healthy ways. I believe we must find ways to disagree without destruction.

Disagreeing in a productive way involves being respectful, open-minded, and focused on finding a solution rather than winning an argument. It's important to start by clearly stating your position and the reasons behind it, and then actively listening to the other person's perspective. Try to understand their point of view and see if there are any areas of common ground. Avoid personal attacks or making assumptions about their intentions. It's also helpful to come up with potential solutions or alternatives that take both parties' concerns into account.

Here are a few tips to help you disagree without damaging your relationship:

Show respect: Avoid personal attacks, name-calling, or any other form of disrespectful behavior.

Communicate clearly: Make sure you understand the other person's perspective and express your own position clearly and calmly. Also, consider that the other person's communication style may be more or less animated than yours. Resist the temptation to regulate their expression. Focus on your ability to stay calm and de-escalate.

Use "I" statements: Instead of accusing the other person, use "I" statements to express your own feelings and concerns. For example, "I feel frustrated when we have this kind of disagreement."

Avoid making assumptions: Don't assume you know what the other person is thinking or feeling. Ask them to explain their perspective. It can be tempting to substitute our judgment of another person's situation for theirs. Don't make assumptions about the other person's intentions or beliefs.

Take responsibility: Own up to your own mistakes and take responsibility for your own actions.

Focus on the issue: Keep the conversation focused on the topic at hand and avoid getting sidetracked by unrelated issues.

Seek common ground: Look for areas of agreement and try to build on those.

Seek solutions: Instead of focusing on winning the argument, focus on finding a solution that works for both parties. Resist the temptation to make the other party a monster. Not every story requires a villain.

Take a break if necessary: If the conversation becomes too heated, it may be best to take a break and come back to the discussion later. I often encourage clients, when possible, to put off conversations they are not mentally ready to hold productively. We all have the capacity to be triggered by challenging conversations.

Be willing to compromise: Be willing to make concessions in order to find a solution that works for both parties. Remember that every relationship requires a give and take, and compromise is a key aspect. By following these guidelines, you will increase the chances of having a productive disagreement that allows the relationship to survive and grow rather than deteriorate.

Chapter 12

Look Out for Potholes

"Vigilance of the wisest kind is to incessantly remain open to the reality that what I 'see' is but a single thread and solitary shard of what 'is.'"

—CRAIG D. LOUNSBROUGH

WHEN I WORKED IN COMMERCIAL REAL ESTATE, THE INDUSTRY was one-half of 1 percent of any ethnic minority. I was the first Black person to have my role in the six-state region in all the top ten companies in the industry. And this is recent history, not in the 1960s.

I was excited to be breaking barriers and opening up a new space for difference in a previously closed industry. The office was organized into open-air cubicle pods. I sat in one with five other White guys. This was my life. I was always surrounded by White guys, I would go to events or conferences with 5,000 people in attendance, and I'd be the only Black person and maybe one of a handful of women in the room. So I got used to that, being surrounded and being the only one in an environment.

And it could be hostile. I was often mistaken for the server or presumed to be the secretary. I once brought a client to an event with me as my guest. We stayed for about an hour but both decided to head out a little early since we had busy days the next morning. We were standing at the valet waiting for our cars. My client was a tall Black man dressed in a suit, and we were engaged in conversation when a White guy in an SUV pulled up to the valet stand and yelled at my client.

"Hey, chief. I'm only going to be in (the event) for a few minutes. Hold my car right here," threw his keys at my client, and ran into the event.

I was mortified. But it wasn't the last time something like that happened. I have more stories than I could recount of the ways I was personally hazed by my "team." But one particular story is burned into my memory.

One day the executive vice president came out of his office to our cubicle pod. He systematically invited literally every single person around me to lunch but me. In front of me. He asked them one at a time, leapfrogging me so intentionally that I felt the exclusion physically in my body. I remember feeling hurt and left out. Again.

Things like this happened to me nearly every day in one way or another. Talk about eroding your spirit. But the thing that's really interesting about this particular story was not the behavior of the EVP but the behavior of my colleagues, my peers that were invited, whom I considered friends.

As the guys got up and started gathering their things to leave the office, they carefully avoided eye contact with me, busying themselves with turning off their computers and putting on their suit jackets. As they scurried out of the office, only one guy turned back and looked at me. In those three seconds, it was clear he knew exactly what was happening. He knew exactly how I felt. And he knew that it wasn't right. I could feel him wanting to do something, mustering a courage he was unable to find.

This young broker was scared. He wasn't the boss. He wasn't the most powerful person in that room, but he still had the power to change the situation. One of the big mistakes we make is we think we have to be the boss to make change. Here's something important, though. You don't have to make the person in charge feel foolish or challenge their authority. He could have simply asked, "Hey, Denise, do you want to come to lunch with us?" Or "Hey, guys, I'll drive so that Denise can come too."

I had spoken with this young man about diversity on many occasions in the past. He was perceptive and often noticed when I was disrespected or treated unfairly. He often said what he would do differently if he was in charge. How, if he were the boss, he would make everyone feel like they belonged. But the amazing opportunity life affords us is that everybody, even the lowest person in the organization, can make everyone feel like they belong.

As we grow and learn how to be Indivisible, we can consume all kinds of information; but at some point we have to start doing. If I want to learn to swim, I can read books about swimming. I can listen to podcasts about swimming. I can even watch videos about swimming. But at some point, I have to actually get in the water and swim.

It can be easy to busy ourselves in the preparation and planning of a task, all the while avoiding the task itself. It's been lovingly referred to as "when I, then I" thinking. When I have sharpened my skills, then I will try. When I learn all the vocabulary words, then I will try to speak the language. It's easy to watch hundreds of painting tutorials on YouTube, but never paint. Ask me how I know. . . .

STOP LOOKING FOR HEAVEN OR HELL

I've learned that before you can heal someone, you have to ask them if they're willing to give up the things that made them sick. There are two challenging populations that threaten our ability to be Indivisible if they don't give up what ails them. The first group thinks America is heaven on Earth. The second group thinks America is an irredeemable hellscape we are barely surviving. Both are problematic.

And they fight. A lot.

We have to guard against the halo and horn effects. The halo effect is a type of cognitive bias that occurs when an overall positive impression of a person or thing leads to an overly favorable evaluation of that person or thing's specific traits and abilities. This occurs because our initial positive impression affects how we perceive and interpret subsequent information about that person or thing.

When it comes to the heaven group, they see America through rose-colored glasses. In their opinion, America can do no wrong. But that's not possible. It's a country run by fallible human beings who make mistakes and sometimes create harm. This group can sometimes take information in and run it through a pixie-dust filter that prevents them from seeing challenges and opportunities for growth. They dismiss legitimate concerns as bellyaching and ingratitude, offering little or no remedy for the problems we objectively have.

The second group—the hellscape folks—isn't any better. They struggle with the opposite problem: the horn effect. This is a cognitive bias where an overall negative impression of a person or thing leads to an overly unfavorable evaluation of that person or thing's specific traits and abilities.

The horn effect can be just as harmful and destructive as the halo effect. This group thinks everything America touches turns to mush. They are unlikely to celebrate any progress at all. This group is quick to offer criticisms, but they never seem to be coupled with actionable solutions. Every day is a bad day and they filter any information they receive through a lens of skepticism and fatalism. They are a lot of fun at parties.

Both the halo and horn effects highlight the importance of being aware of our own biases. Both of these groups have been responsible for the sabotage of imagination. If we reject any negative information we receive as unpatriotic and disrespectful, then we won't be able to make America better. You can't fix a problem you don't acknowledge.

But the flip side is equally true. We can't reject America either, refusing to be a part of what's possible for the future. If you're locked in disappointment with what is going wrong, it can rob you of the creativity and optimism needed to forge a new future.

Being Indivisible requires both of these groups to put down their biases and work to operate in truth. America isn't heaven or hell. It's ours. We need to work together every day to make it the best it can be for all of us.

BEWARE OF LESSER GOALS

"We are kept from our goals not by obstacles, but by a clear path to a lesser goal."

—ROBERT BRAULT

I am obsessed with turtles. My husband and I went to Florida for a visit. This was during the time of year when the mama turtles come on shore, crawl their way up onto the sand, lay their eggs, and then go back into the water. There are literal drones that fly over the shoreline to mark where the eggs are so that they can be protected, because they're an endangered species.

Miami-Dade County's Sea Turtle Conservation Program tracks when those eggs are going to hatch and deploy teams to make sure all of the turtles make it to the water. So we were sitting there in the dark, watching the little babies hatch. When the babies come up, you wonder, "How do they know what to do?" They're only three minutes old. How do they know to go to the water? They've never even seen water. Well, they instinctively move toward the moonlight reflecting off the water. Genius design.

But the moonlight isn't the only light on the Florida coastline. Restaurants and hotels all along the beach cast a distracting glow. Artificial lights cause problems for hatchlings as they emerge from their nests at night and instinctively crawl toward the direction of the brightest light. These lights cause them to crawl inland and away from the ocean, or to wander aimlessly on the beach, burning up energy that is important for their survival if they do reach the sea. Disoriented hatchlings often die from dehydration, exhaustion, being attacked or eaten, and even being crushed in traffic.

So we worked all night turning those babies around. Sometimes you pick them up and turn them around and they are so confused that they turn back again toward the street, so you have to pick them up and turn them around again. It's not an obstacle to the goal that is the problem. It's the ease of that lesser goal.

It is tempting to focus on the smallest elements or the lowest-hanging fruit when contemplating challenging problems. One great example of this is the stranger danger PSAs of the 1980s and 1990s, which aimed to teach children about how to protect themselves from child sexual abuse. This messaging was popular in the United States and elsewhere, and came from numerous organizations and programs. Every child of the era was drilled to avoid talking to or accepting gifts from strangers and to immediately report any suspicious behavior to a trusted adult—a sentiment succinctly captured on the popular children's show *Barney & Friends*:

> Never talk to strangers
> That's very good advice.
> 'Cause you just can't tell
> If they're good or bad,
> Even though they may seem nice.
> Even though they may seem nice.
> Don't get in their car (No, no!)
> Don't take anything from them (No, no!)
> Just turn around (Yeah!)
> And walk away (Yeah!)
> Go back and tell a grownup friend! (Oh yeah!)
> Go back and tell a grownup friend!

By any objective measure, the campaign effectively achieved its goal to warn children about the threat of strangers. There's only one problem. The vast majority of child sexual assault is committed by someone known to the child. The program focused on the tiniest sliver of the problem, leaving the lion's share completely unaddressed. While children were being taught to watch out for strangers who coincidentally looked different from them, they were being assaulted by priests, sports coaches, relatives, and camp counselors. According to the Rape, Abuse & Incest National Network (RAINN), the majority of child and teen victims know the perpetrator.[64] Of sexual abuse cases reported to law enforcement, 93 percent of juvenile victims knew the assailant: 59 percent were acquaintances and 34 percent were family members. Only 7 percent were strangers to the victim.

By failing to focus on the true bad actors, we essentially miseducated an entire generation of children. Teaching xenophobia rather than self advocacy and boundaries with the adults in their lives. The campaign may have also hindered children's ability to distinguish between trustworthy and untrustworthy individuals and made it harder for them to seek help from strangers in emergency situations.

Adequate and accurate definition of any problem is critical. I understand why this approach was taken. It is incredibly difficult to overcome the social mores governing adults and children in our culture. We see this in the resistance to the gentle parenting movement. One of the tenets of the movement is that children have the agency to set boundaries in their physical interactions. Plainly put, if little Johnny doesn't want to hug Uncle Joe, he is not forced to do so. There has been quite a bit of resistance to this by older relatives feeling that this boundary is disrespectful and children should be compelled to greet their relatives affectionately. But considering the statistics, if little Johnny's instincts are telling them not to kiss or hug Uncle Joe, we should honor that. Nevertheless, it provides a challenge. We have not been ready to empower children to set boundaries with the adults in their lives. So in lieu of being able to address the problem directly, the creators of this program simply chose a lesser goal.

I see it in my work often. A company gets feedback that they do not have adequate diverse representation in their leadership, so they quickly announce an internship program recruiting at HBCUs That solution solves *a* problem, but not *the* problem. Indivisible leaders have the courage to apply the solutions necessary to create actual change.

Chapter 13

Widen Your Aperture

"You can observe a lot just by watching."

—YOGI BERRA

THROUGHOUT MY CAREER, ONE OF THE SERVICES I HAVE PROVIDED is helping CEOs craft messages for their employees. This is one of my favorite things to do because I get to spend time with these pivotal leaders and I get to see firsthand how sincere and passionate they are about making their teams Indivisible. Once, I was prepping a CEO to address his entire employee base of 24,000 employees. The address was a town hall–style gathering and we were reviewing his responses to some of the questions the employees had submitted.

He was doing well. His answer to the first question was thoughtful. The second? Understanding. But his answer to the third question surprised us all.

"What do you think is the most impactful thing that you saw in the murder of George Floyd?"

He answered, "Well, the fact that nobody stopped to help; everybody was filming. I can't believe nobody tried to intervene."

I cleared the room of other staff to speak with him privately. When educating someone, humiliation is not required. Embarrassment is not an effective tool for educating people, especially leaders. We don't have to make people small to help them grow.

I said, "Sir, I'm sorry, that's not true."

At first he argued with me. "What do you mean? Everybody was just filming, like, nobody tried to help."

He didn't believe me so I pulled out my phone and showed him the other bystander videos. I showed him the multiple people screaming and begging for the police to stop. I showed him the police pointing their guns at people who were trying to intervene. I showed him people inconsolable as they saw the life draining from George's body. He was horrified.

He had been fully prepared to say something to his entire organization that was categorically false. He had been so sure of what he thought. And it was not right. He had received his information from only one source and trusted it entirely.

This was unusual behavior for a CEO. Usually, leaders try to gather as much information as possible when making critical decisions. Let's say you were going to open a branch of your business in Brazil. Not only would you research the business dynamics, but you would also research the culture. You would engage people who speak the languages. You would explore the political environment and cultural practices. There is no way you would rely on one source for all of your information.

Unfortunately, we do not always apply this rigor to our private lives. Not only do we consume information in limited places but we rarely validate the information we are exposed to. We have to develop the courage and the skills to fact-check the information we're given today.

EAT A BALANCED DIET

David was brilliant. He was one of the most interesting people I had ever met. He taught artificial intelligence at the PhD level at the world's most prestigious technology departments in Hong Kong and California. We were engaged in a thoughtful group discussion about censorship with people from several different countries. The Americans in the conversation were railing against China and the way it limited information that their citizens had access to. The conversation went on for several minutes before David weighed in. He said, "It is interesting to hear your judgment about censorship when the United States is the most algorithmically censored place on Earth."

As his comment hung in the air, I was struck by its deep profundity. As much as I hated to admit it, he was right. We are locked in profit-driven echo chambers, being force-fed one-sided narratives, outrage, and misinformation.

And some of us don't even know it.

The algorithms direct us to movies and TV shows like the ones we've enjoyed in the past, suggest products that we can't live without, and point us to the exact right kitten videos that will leave us on the floor in stitches. But algorithms can also spread misinformation.

Misinformation and disinformation have had a significant impact on political campaigns in the United States in recent years, particularly in the context of social media and the internet. The spread of false or misleading information can shape public opinion and influence voting behavior, potentially undermining the integrity of elections. The use of social media and other digital tools to amplify and spread disinformation has made it easier for American politics to be manipulated. This has led to increased concern about the role of disinformation and misinformation in political campaigns and calls for greater efforts to combat these issues.

There are numerous impacts that must be guarded against:

Undermining of democracy and the integrity of elections: Misinformation and disinformation can shape public opinion and influence voting behavior, potentially undermining the integrity of elections and democratic processes.

Public health risks: Misinformation and disinformation about health and medical issues can lead to harm, such as people avoiding vaccinations or rejecting proven treatments.

Economic harm: Misinformation and disinformation can impact financial markets, business decisions, and consumer behavior, leading to economic losses.

Social harm: Misinformation and disinformation can fuel social divisions, prejudice, and discrimination.

Confusion and mistrust: Misinformation and disinformation can create confusion and mistrust, making it difficult for individuals and communities to make informed decisions and trust in public institutions.

Security risks: Misinformation and disinformation can be used as a tool by hostile actors to interfere with politics, create chaos, and undermine national security.

Misinformation and disinformation can be very deceiving and can spread far more quickly than truth, so we all must play a part in shutting down falsehoods, especially in a midterm election year.

- 80 percent of US adults have consumed fake news.
- 67 percent of US adults have read false information on social media.
- 64 percent of US adults believe that fabricated information causes much confusion about basic facts of current issues.
- 86 percent of internet users admit to being duped by fake news.
- Americans believe that 61 percent of news on social media contains misinformation.[65]

Many of us hope that people are capable of sifting through a mountain of data to discern the truth, but how can this happen when the truth isn't even in the pile they are given? Or when there's only half the story?

What you consume matters. Messages matter. The total advertising expenditure in the United States is $345.3 billion per year. Coca-Cola alone spends $4.25 billion worldwide on advertising.

Those dollars are spent to capture attention and influence choices. Our attention is the currency of this age. Unfortunately, there are many incentives to give us pieces of the truth, as well as outright lies. Peter Sandergaard said, "The amount of data being generated is growing faster than our ability to analyze it." The challenge we face is to extract meaning from a world overwhelmed by information.

This leaves us with a critical responsibility to examine where we get our stories and to develop a discipline around verifying our information as well as to make sure we have all the information necessary to form an opinion.

We can start by examining where we get our stories. You can start by listing your primary and secondary sources of information and ask yourself some hard questions:

- What information outlets do you trust?
- Why do you trust them?
- What is their process for verifying what they share?
- Have they been credibly accused of sharing disinformation?
- Do they skew toward your political belief system?
- Do they platform outlier conspiracies?
- Do you reject content if it comes from a site that isn't politically aligned with you?
- What sources do you avoid?
- Do you know how to evaluate the credibility of the sources you use?
- In the rush to get the story first, do they often make mistakes that require retraction?
- How loudly are retractions shared? Do they accept responsibility when they get it wrong?
- Do you read the book or listen to what someone tells you the book says?
- Do they have notable omissions? Are they fair about what they choose to cover as well as what they exclude in coverage?
- Do they catastrophize the news inappropriately?

Indivisible leaders are well-informed leaders. It is virtually impossible to effectively lead diverse teams if your information diet is not well-rounded and credible.

CHECK THE RECEIPTS

Even after you identify the outlets you deem trust-worthy, you still need a process to verify the information. This is particularly true on the internet. As you know, not all information online is accurate or reliable. There is a lot of misinformation, propaganda, and outright false information on the internet, and if you don't verify the information you're reading, you risk spreading that misinformation or basing your beliefs or actions on false information. Stephen Hawking said, "The volume of information is increasing exponentially, while our ability to understand it is not."

Additionally, fact-checking helps you to think critically about the information you consume, and to understand the context in which it was created and presented. By fact-checking, you can gain a deeper understanding of the topic at hand and make more informed decisions. False information can be spread deliberately, for example as a form of propaganda or political manipulation, or accidentally, through the simple act of sharing information without verifying its accuracy.

It's important to know how to fact-check and where to find reliable sources, doing that you can make sure you have an accurate understanding.

Some reliable sources for fact-checking are:
- **PolitiFact:** A fact-checking website that rates the accuracy of claims by elected officials and others on its Truth-O-Meter.
- **Snopes:** The definitive internet reference source for researching urban legends, folklore, myths, rumors, and misinformation.
- **FactCheck.org:** A website that performs fact-checking, affiliated with the Annenberg Public Policy Center of the University of Pennsylvania. Its purpose is to "monitor the factual accuracy" in

American politics by focusing on statements made by US politicians. The group employs a number of journalists who research material.

- **SciCheck:** FactCheck.org's SciCheck feature focuses exclusively on false and misleading scientific claims that are made by partisans to influence public policy.
- **FlackCheck:** This site provides resources designed to help viewers recognize flaws in arguments in general and political ads in particular. Video resources point out deception and incivility in political rhetoric.

Part 4

LISTEN FOR ECHOES

Chapter 14

Look for Breadcrumbs

"The past will often attack the present with the pain of your memories."
—SEIICHI KIRIMA

THOMAS WAS INCREDIBLY ANNOYED WITH ME.

"It's discriminatory," I said.

"What are you talking about?!? It's just a minute. Is everything racist with you people?"

Thomas and I had met at a cocktail party for a major tech conference. He introduced himself as the principal in charge of the conference's pitch competition. When I heard that I had the internal struggle I often have; do I tell him?

When you see things happening in the world that are problematic, it can be a difficult choice to speak up. But as usual, I decided to go for it.

"I noticed that you changed the amount of time allocated to the startups to pitch from three minutes to two minutes. Have you ever considered that your rule change discriminates against women and people of color?"

Thomas rolled his eyes. It wasn't a reaction I was unfamiliar with. In my experience, people often say they are open to feedback, but rarely are.

"Please. Tell me, Denise. How are we discriminating?" in a tone that did not suggest he was interested in my answer.

I gave him my answer anyway. When you share cultural norms

and experiences, you develop a shorthand. Your common cultural or experiential history provides a foundation to communicate faster. For example, if I am a man pitching a panel of male judges a business about dry cleaning men's shirts, I don't have to explain that the dry cleaning comes on disposable hangers or that it is wrapped in plastic or that the shirts have buttons. Those facts are understood. Contrast that with an Asian woman explaining eyelid tape to that same panel of male judges. She will have to explain what eyelid tapes are, what they look like, how they are used, etc. before she can even get to the point of stating the problem and her solution. She needs more time.

Thomas looked at me dumbfounded. That had never occurred to him. He went on to say that the judges had been complaining that they were having trouble evaluating some of the startups because even if they listened to the whole pitch, they still didn't understand what the problem being solved was.

They had been attributing this understanding gap to the people pitching instead of the disadvantage created by the rule change.

This, my friends, is an echo.

PHYSICAL ENVIRONMENT

Echoes are all around us. Echoes are remnants of old harms. If we want to be Indivisible, we are all going to have to get better at identifying the subtle ways legacy exclusion and preferential treatment show up in our everyday practices. We must decouple malice and harm. Sometimes, no harm is intended, but old stories do not release us easily. Remnants of old harms can show up in innocuous places. It is our job to look.

I was doing a sound check for a speech I would be doing at a conference. We checked the lighting and the microphones, but as I walked around the stage, my heels fell through the slats connecting the planks that formed it. It was a problem I had never encountered before, but one I had to speak up about because it was a trip hazard, and I had no intention of face-planting in front of an audience of 1,000 people. When I asked if there was anything we could do about it, the tech laughed and said he wasn't sure. I was the first woman to ever speak at that conference. They had never had to fix that problem because they had never had that problem. An echo.

When my daughter was little, she took a ballet class. As the troupe prepared for their recital the leader sent a letter home with instructions. The girls were asked to pull their hair into a tight bun for the performance. While my daughter had hair suited for that, another Black girl in the class did not. Her mother called me distraught because her daughter (who just happened to be the best dancer in the class) was distraught and wanted to quit ballet because she didn't think she would fit in.

Of course that was not what the troupe leader wanted. She hadn't given any thought at all to the differences in the girls' hair. She had literally just photocopied the instructions she had given out the year before.

Our goal as leaders is to create the best possible environment for the best dancers to dance. To do so, we must watch for echoes.

There are more statues of Confederacy figures in public spaces than there are of women.

We still fund public schools based on property taxes.

Cash bail frees the rich while imprisoning the poor, irrespective of guilt or innocence.

Echoes.

RULES

In my work, I have seen so many damaging, limiting rules:

- We only recruit at these three colleges.
- You must have AP classes to apply for this school, even if your high school does not offer them.
- You must have X experience to be considered for this position, but women are restricted from those feeder positions.
- You must be an accredited investor to invest in tech startups, or you will miss this modern-day gold rush. (Oddly, you can gamble at the casino as much as you want, but not invest in your future.)

- You must wear your hair like X, but that is not how it grows out of your head.
- To make partner, you must have X years of uninterrupted work with the firm, with no exceptions for maternity leave.
- You must pay $X to get out of jail, before you can even be proven guilty or innocent, even if you are poor. Under this model, a guilty rich person can be at home sleeping comfortably in their own bed while an innocent poor person sleeps in a cell for years awaiting trial.

Rules can be treacherous. They can provide order, but they can also codify discrimination and exclusion. We must explore their effect and be honest about their cause.

Do your rules penalize caregivers? Exclude those from different religions? Arbitrarily dictate physical requirements that restrict people with disabilities? Do they devalue people from low socioeconomic backgrounds? We must explore the ways rules can be weaponized and manipulated to stamp out differences and maintain the status quo. We must also dismantle the ones that hurt our ability to move forward together.

Part of that work is to articulate unwritten rules. Navigating unspoken expectations and boundaries can be extremely draining for people new to an environment. Make every effort to clearly articulate the rules you expect the person to operate under, even if they seem simple and obvious to you.

SYSTEMS

One of the hardest things to do is to pan back and examine systems that need to change. There is quite a bit of scrutiny being given to the important task of rooting out harm, but far less to remove preferential treatment.

Let's use the path of a tenant rep broker in the commercial real estate business as an example.

Two people start in commercial real estate at the same time.

Jason: A White C student whose father is friends with the highest-earning brokers in the office.

Lisa: A Black woman who is bright, but has no relationships or experience in the industry

Both are welcomed into the office, but Jason is added to the high-producer team. As a result, he is given one-half of 1 percent of the deals his team does. At his minimal level, all he does is make copies and grab coffee.

Lisa is not added to any team. She has to catch, kill, skin, and cook every deal she gets all on her own.

Fast forward four years, and let's compare resumes. Jason's resume says he has worked numerous deals of 200,000 square feet or more. Lisa has done every aspect of her deals, but as a junior broker working solo, her deals are much smaller at 5,000 square feet or 7,500 square feet. You get the idea.

Lisa is far more knowledgeable than Jason, but his resume has been amplified to position him for future opportunities Lisa will never have access to.

It's important to note that this disparity is really no individual person's fault. The system itself creates inequity. Is it any surprise that commercial real estate is one of the least diverse industries in the country?

•

We do not have a good track record of addressing the negative impact of privilege, even when it seems obvious.

During Jeffrey Dahmer's first trial for brutally attacking and lobotomizing a young boy, the judge gave him a shockingly lenient sentence. He said it was because Jeffrey reminded him of his grandson. He did not feel that Jeffrey Dahmer was the kind of person who goes to prison. He "deserved" a second chance. Dahmer went on to torture, kill, and cannibalize seventeen men and boys.

In the Brock Turner case, Judge Aaron Persky said that, although

Brock had been caught in the act of brutally raping an unconscious woman behind a dumpster, he thought Turner would "not be a danger to others" and expressed concern that "a prison sentence would have a severe impact" on him.

Who we limit is one problem. But who we elevate and protect is an entirely different issue that requires our attention and remediation. We don't always talk about the harm of positive biases. But we should.

Chapter 15

Fight Homeostasis

"What you do every day matters more than
what you do once in a while."

—GRETCHEN RUEBEN

TAKE A STROLL WITH ME BACK TO NINTH GRADE BIOLOGY. HOPE-
fully, you remember homeostasis, the state of steady internal conditions maintained by living systems. In other words, the processes that
keep things normal, average. In a cell, water and nutrients are let in and
waste and toxins are let out to maintain a steady normal state. Our bodies operate in the same way. When your body is hot, you sweat. When
you are cold, you shiver. Everything works to keep you average, regular.

I believe every system in the world works like this. Conditions are
altered to maintain the status quo because it is comfortable, familiar,
and it feels safe.

But what happens when you want to do something extraordinary?
When you want to break the rules and push the boundaries? What
happens then?

Lindsay had spent her career working toward the goal of being in
the C suite of the energy industry. As my client, Lindsay was singular
in her focus. She was disciplined, focused, and committed to excellence. She aligned everything in her life toward her goal. I was sure she
would reach it.

Because the energy industry is multinational, international assign-
ments are a key stepping stone in the journey to executive leadership.

It would be ridiculous to try to run an international company if you only have domestic experience. Lindsay had made it clear to her superiors that she was ready and willing to take that next big step.

Finally, the call came. Lindsay's voicemail to me was beyond excited. She had received a two-year assignment in the Middle East. During this project, she was going to learn, grow her skills, and blow them away. Then, she planned to come back to the States and make her own personal hole in the glass ceiling. It was going to be incredible.

You can imagine the smile that crossed my lips as I listened to her message. She was so happy, and I was unbelievably proud. I called her back immediately, but I was shocked by our exchange.

"Hi, Lindsay."

"Hi," she said mopily.

"Congratulations! I'm so excited for you."

"Thanks. But I'm not sure I'm going to take it."

I was stunned. She had left her excited message less than one hour before. What could have possibly happened in that short amount of time to change her mind?

The answer? She had called her mother. You can imagine what Mom said. Is it safe? Won't you be lonely? How are you going to date? What if you wait too late to have kids? Are you sure this is a good decision?

Here Lindsay was, poised to do something extraordinary, and her own mother planted the seeds of doubt. As Lindsay prepared to leave what was "normal," she was pulled back to the "regular" path. There is no doubt that her mother loved her, but in a way, her mother's love actually became her cage.

Some of the changes we will make in an effort to be Indivisible will not be comfortable. They may feel alien, and we might be tempted to long for "old normal" no matter how toxic those times may have been. Do not be lulled. Learn to name homeostasis and to call it out when you are tempted to regress in the face of progress.

If we do not budget for the forces that will come against change, we greatly put our capacity for change at risk. We do not want to be average, normal, or regular. We want to be extraordinary.

Fight homeostasis.

BEWARE OF THE NORM

Tammy's son Chad played in an elite suburban soccer league. The league was pursuing some governmental funding to retrofit their fields but was receiving criticism because there was no diversity on the team. The parents were asked to meet to with the athletic director to discuss some ideas to address the issue. Tammy didn't really understand what the problem was. As she drove around their small community, she often saw incredibly talented kids from communities of color playing soccer. Why couldn't they just update their recruiting? She was eager to attend the meeting and get to the bottom of the issue.

As they gathered in the team office, the athletic director talked for twenty minutes, and Tammy still didn't understand the challenge. Finally, she raised her hand and asked, "Why can't we just recruit some of these great kids that play at Tinsley [a neighborhood park]? They are super talented. Surely, we can just give a few scholarships to the right talent, right? WIN WIN!"

But it was clear that others in the room were uneasy and did not agree with Tammy's simple solution. The group took a ten-minute break. While Tammy was grabbing her coffee, she asked the soccer coach what the big deal was.

He said "Tammy, you don't get it. No one in this room is going to say it out loud. Rich parents don't pay for their kids to sit on the bench. They pay for their kids to play. If they let all these other kids in, then their kids won't be the stars anymore."

Tammy was horrified. Weeks later, as she recounted this story to me, she said it in hushed tones, as if it were a deep, dark secret trust she was broaching.

Creative ideas and solutions are often presented, but there are always parties committed to the status quo. It's easier to keep things the way they are. That's why learning to identify and fight homeostasis is so important.

•

In my work with women, I often get the opportunity to interview executive women about the challenges they experience as they climb the corporate ladder. They share many issues with me: trouble getting credit for their ideas, difficulty maintaining boundaries, executive presence, among others. As an executive woman myself, most of their experiences are expected and analogous to my own. But there is one challenge I have experienced personally that I was shocked to hear from women over and over again.

Assistants often treat women differently than men.

A thirty-year-old woman gets promoted to a leadership role in a law firm. She is one of four lawyers who share an assistant. That assistant is a forty-eight-year-old woman who has been working with the three other male attorneys for two years. Whenever the newly promoted attorney asks the assistant to perform a task, the assistant prioritizes the men's requests. "You know how helpless they are. They can't function without me. I'll get to your request when I can."

A thirty-three-year-old woman joins a finance team as a managing director. Her assistant schedules a meeting to train the executive on how to enter her own time sheets and expense reports because, she says, the director is tech savvy and she's "sure you don't need me to do that."

A forty-year-old woman earns the role of managing director of a firm. The team has a potluck lunch to celebrate a coworker's retirement. After the party, the managing director heads back to her office to start returning calls when her assistant knocks on the door to ask if she is going to help clean up. She says, "It will really do a lot for morale for the other assistants to see that you are one of the team." Of course, the same invitation was not offered to any of the male executives.

I interviewed some assistants to ask about this phenomenon and their answers were enlightening:

- "It's hard not to think of the executive like a niece or a daughter."
- "Other women just get it. We don't have to be as formal or as serious as we do with the guys."
- "The guys just need more help. The women are so much more capable."
- "She can usually figure things out on her own."
- "I guess I think of her more as one of the girls. She is just like us."

In a way, the assistants in these scenarios are the keepers of the status quo. They themselves were not ready for the very necessary change of increased female leadership. Through their behavior, the assistants were asking the question "Who does she think she is?"

Homeostasis tells us we're going too far before we have even started.

Another place homeostasis rears its ugly head is in catastrophizing the possibilities. We often hear questions like: What if it goes too far? When is it too much? Where does it stop? I ask, "Where does it start?" We are surrounded by results that are statistically impossible without manipulation of the systems. We are not in danger of overreach.

We've all been taught to treat others the way we want to be treated, but I think we misapply that lesson. A ficus and a cactus are both plants. They both require water, but to give the same amount to both is a death sentence to one. Instead of giving them the *same* amount of water, we have to give each the water they need. We must be creative and develop more sophisticated solutions. There is no one-size-fits-all.

DON'T RUN OUT OF GAS

When you are in the midst of change it can be easy to lose sight of the goal. When people are resistant to change, they will frame the problem in such a way as to either show that the problem never really existed or that the problem has been solved and no additional intervention is required. These messages can be tempting. Don't let people talk you out of progress.

After the televised murder of George Floyd, there were many calls to reform the police. Some even called for the police to be defunded. But that's not what happened.

Not only were the police not defunded, but 90 percent of cities and counties *increased* police funding between the fiscal years 2018–19 and 2021–22. Of the 10 percent of agencies that did decrease funding, the cuts were small, with only eight agencies trimming the budget by more than 2 percent, an amount many local government budget experts deemed irrelevant.[66]

Increased funding in and of itself is not necessarily problematic—if it is generating improved results. But that also isn't true.

US law enforcement killed at least 1,176 people in 2022, making it the deadliest year on record for police violence since experts first started tracking these killings.[67]

We all want change, but we are not demanding accountability for change.

How do we do this in our lives? In my work, I see many leadership teams back down when team members push back on their commitment to inclusion. The loudest squeaky wheel gets to drive the agenda. I will say to you what I say to them: Leadership takes vision and commitment to that vision. We must have the courage to follow through with our culture change. Lack of commitment leads to lack of success. Then that lack of performance is used as an excuse to kill the program.

A client I had been working with for a few months reached out to me for counsel about a situation that had developed. They had recently made an offer to a candidate for a manager role. The candidate accepted the offer but had one caveat to his acceptance of the position. Because of recent news about the #MeToo movement, he was unwilling to meet with any women employees alone. He was willing to meet with the male employees he would be supervising, even have meals or engage in activities outside the office with them, but he could not do that with any female employee.

The client asked me what I thought. As you can probably imagine, I had many thoughts and none of them were good.

"Let me get this straight," I said. "You have a position managing people. This applicant has told you, in the interview, that he is only willing to manage half of the people under his charge. He is only willing to do half of his job."

The client responded, "Well, when you say it like that it sounds ridiculous. You're right. We've been spending time and energy trying to make our organizations more equitable and inclusive. Why would we hire someone who is actively telling us he isn't willing to be either? I don't even know why we called you. Thank you for your time."

Change takes stamina and sometimes we have to find choke points to remind us what our objectives are.

Now, before you judge them, I want to celebrate the fact that they called. They knew they were in murky territory and they leveraged our relationship to validate what they already knew to be true. I count that as a victory and tip my hat to them. I wish more organizations had the courage to ask for help when they needed it. It can be uncomfortable to apply new principles to old processes. But growth and comfort do not coexist. Growth can be painful, but nothing is as painful as staying in a condition you don't belong in. Not every step you take will be forward, but you must stay committed to the goal.

The most dangerous time for the space shuttle is the reentry. You would think flying hundreds of miles above the Earth would be the hard part, but it's actually takeoff and reentry that are the most dangerous. What are the points in your life that provide the biggest threats to progress?

STAY COACHABLE

It is important to remember that each and every one of us has an important part to play in inclusion. We have to stay open, positive, and coachable. I have a dear friend who was a bit of a phenom and was promoted to administration of a college at a very young age. He was Black and, at twenty-eight, was the youngest administrator by fifteen years. He was an intellectual heavyweight, but a bit insecure about his age, so he thought he would grow a beard. It was tragic, a truly AWFUL beard. Terrible. One of the Black employees at the college pulled him to the side and told him it wasn't working. He got an E for effort, but it wasn't giving him the mature effect he was going for. He cut the beard off. When he told me this story, I asked him "Could a White guy have told you that?" He thought about it and said maybe not. He might have been offended.

Now that's a problem. We have to stay coachable. People have to be able to help us grow and develop into mature leaders. We are asking allies to speak up, but we also have to be willing to listen. We have to create the space for true authentic dialogue. That's the only way we will grow. We have to be able to receive hard truths designed to help us move to the next level. Sometimes that will be uncomfortable, but we have to try to ascribe good intent and stay open. We never step into the same river twice. We have to resist the temptation to operate in mistrust and bring the baggage of past disappointments to every interaction. We have to be willing to start fresh. To give people an authentic chance to mentor and develop us when appropriate. We don't have to have a female mentor because we are women or a Latino mentor because we are Hispanic. We have to be open to people who are willing to help and know the path forward. That's the big part we ALL play in creating an inclusive culture.

Chapter 16

Choose Justice Over Peace

*"We can choose courage or we can choose comfort,
but we can't have both."*

—BRENÉ BROWN

A GROUP OF EMPLOYEES IS GATHERED IN A CONFERENCE ROOM waiting for a meeting to start. The room is buzzing with excitement because there have been three recent resignations and retirements in leadership positions. Everyone is wondering who will be tapped for the opportunities to move up in the organization. As they grab their coffee, they start talking about it.

Paloma, the only Hispanic woman on the team, shares that she would love to have the opportunity to have the director role.

Jim says, "Now, Paloma, you know you don't really want that job. You know you would much rather be home having some anchor babies." The room freezes, but no one says anything. Paloma is obviously offended and tells Jim, "That's not an appropriate comment." To which Jim responds, "Don't get mad. You know how you fiery Latinas get." Paloma says, "Jim, enough, this conversation is ending right now."

Someone reports to the boss that Jim and Paloma "were fighting" before the meeting. Several attendees of the meeting approach Paloma after and express how sorry they are and offer comments like, "You know how Jim is" and that he was out of line.

The boss calls both Jim and Paloma in and says, "I understand the two of you are not getting along. Harmony and cooperation are really important to me. I hope you can put your heads together and figure out how to resolve this."

Where did it all go wrong?

Jim was way out of line.

When he was called out, he doubled down.

None of the coworkers spoke up.

After the meeting, people approached Paloma to soothe themselves, not Paloma. This came across as personal brand management. They don't want Paloma to think they are like Jim.

Nobody had the courage to speak up in the meeting, but they inaccurately reported back to the boss that there was a "conflict," leaving out the fact that Jim had been the bad actor.

The supervisor didn't investigate the incident for himself. Instead, he divided the responsibility for the conflict between Jim and Paloma when she bore no responsibility for the incident. He basically assigned the task of addressing the behavior of Jim to Jim's subordinate, Paloma. What authority does she have to compel change?

When an incident like this takes place, people often say, "It's not that big of a deal, it will blow over." They are not right about that. There are countless consequences when situations like this are mishandled.

Here are just a few:
- Jim is emboldened and his behavior, unchecked, gets worse.
- Paloma no longer trusts the boss or the rest of the team.
- She starts looking for another job.
- Paloma is in extremely high demand because she is talented yet part of a group that is underrepresented in the industry. Where she previously ignored recruiters' calls, she is now starting to take them.
- People share this story on the office grapevine, and it becomes company lore: yet more proof that this company does not support non-White employees.
- Other non-White employees observe this situation and start to lose trust in the team.

- They start looking for other positions as well. I am of true
- Since the company won't address Jim's inappropriate behavior, angry employees start setting a firmer boundary with Jim and handling him aggressively, because they are not going to allow him to treat them like he treated Paloma.
- Those employees are chastised for being combative and intemperate. Always so angry . . .
- Employees exposed to this situation rate the company poorly at online workplace-rating sites, damaging the company's external brand and making recruiting top performers more difficult.
- Leaders push back on diversity goals and give up on trying to increase the diversity of the team because there are "no good applicants." It's "too hard to recruit them" and "they just don't stay."

All because the supervisor chose peace over justice. It can be easier to overlook bad behavior. No one wants conflict. But when bad behavior goes unchecked, the ripples go much further than we anticipate. Comfort-seeking avoidance may save some energy today, but it is often far more expensive in the long run.

WE DON'T EVEN MAKE THAT CHOICE FOR OURSELVES

When my daughter was in the second grade, I was driving on a two-lane country highway in Texas when I saw police lights in my rear-view mirror. I knew I wasn't speeding. That's not my particular brand of adventure. I pulled over and a lone officer approached my car. My sleepy second grader was passed out in the back seat. The next simple request was one every Black person fears. The officer asked me to step out of my car. A wave of panic washed over me. I asked him why I was being stopped, but he ignored my question.

With little alternative, I did the only thing I could do on the side of a dark country road: I complied. That's what you do when you want to make it home. You comply.

He then asked me if he could search my car. I knew his request was unlawful. I had done nothing wrong, and he had not indicated anything to the contrary. But, like I have been required to do so many other times in this body, I traded my liberty for my safety and the safety of my child. I looked at my daughter, now awake, groggy, and totally terrified. And I complied.

His next request took my breath away—since he was illegally searching my car while alone, he needed us to lie face down in the dirt for HIS safety.

Let's review:
- He had the authority.
- He had the gun.
- He had the ability to call down an army of backup that would shoot first and ask questions later based on his word alone.
- But he was afraid . . . of us.

Me. And my sleepy second grader.

I was horrified. And angry. And humiliated. I wanted to fight. I wanted to resist. I wanted to meet the violence of his request with violence of my own. As my daughter began to cry, I imagined what my resistance would cost her. How easily this situation could escalate to me being arrested, brutalized, or even killed. My daughter could not be in foster care in this brutal little town. Not in the hands of these people.

So I complied.

It was amazing how quickly the calculation of the decision happened in my head. Seconds really. Years of making such unholy bargains had developed a musculature in me that often broke my spirit but kept me alive.

So we did it. We held hands and locked eyes and laid face down on the ground. The dirt ruining my daughter's pretty little yellow sundress made her cry even harder. I looked at her and said, "It will be OK."

In other words, I lied. It was not OK.

He searched my car, found nothing, and mumbled that I was free to go. I slowly got up, as he was still a threat, and dusted off our clothes. I wished it was as easy to clean the hurt and anger from my spirit.

It wasn't.

I carried it with me to work the next day. I remember feeling so disconnected from my coworkers. The incident had changed me. How could they be smiling and cracking jokes when I felt so damaged?

Experiences like this change you. They can teach you to limit yourself, always trying to comply in order to seek safety. That same behavior has manifested for me at work more times than I can remember. For example, I was the first and only Black person in my role at a commercial real estate firm, one of the top ten companies in our six-state region. I was hazed mercilessly throughout my time at this firm, but one particular experience has never left me. A senior leader in the firm called me into his office for a chat. He liked me, he said, and thought I was wicked smart; maybe the smartest in the office. "But, Denise," he told me, "a Black person can't make it in this business." He then offered me a piece of career advice: "You should go learn to make the flyers and the banners like Sara, the marketing girl. Everyone needs flyers and banners."

As I sat there in stunned silence, I knew I had three choices:

- I could fly into a rage—and I had every right to. What he said was horrifically offensive. But then I would have been labeled the angry Black woman.
- I could have cried, because what he said hurt me deeply, but then I would have validated his belief that women weren't tough enough for this business.
- Or I could keep my eyes on my own goals, stand up, thank him for his feedback, and walk out gracefully, which is what I did.

I wish I could say I even contemplated a fourth choice: Explain to him how hurtful and racist his words were. At that point in my tenure with the company, countless incidents of hazing and disrespect had depleted me. I simply did not have the energy left to educate him. To put my hand in the proverbial tiger's mouth by risking yet another careless rejection of my humanity. Victims of exclusion are not always in a position to educate their assailants.

As had been required so many times in my career, I was forced to pull on the musculature of maladaptation. Performing the instant calculations necessary for survival and, once again, assuming the management of the casual violence of others. I have been rewarded because I have learned to adapt to toxicity. But it's simplistic to think there was no cost for his behavior. He didn't just hurt my feelings; he hurt the bottom line. Introducing the toxic distraction of racism is just a waste of energy, gifts, and power. It cheats us out of the strength we could have together. I look at what I was able to achieve despite him and imagine what I could have achieved with his support.

Indivisible leaders are sensitive to situations that waste the valuable talent of each contributor. They set boundaries and hold them to create optimal conditions for success.

RIGHT AND "RIGHTER"

I'm fascinated by the cannabis industry in America today. The overwhelming majority of the executives in that industry are White men.[68] Do you think none of those guys ever smoked weed until it was legal? Of course they did. That's why they are experts on weed.

So let me get this straight. One group smokes weed, they lose their freedom, their educational opportunities, their employment opportunities, and, in some cases, their families. The other group smokes weed, and they go on to be millionaires.

As people flock to these industries, more and more are examining their values. They are challenged by the irony that thousands of people are sitting in jail for the very business they're pursuing. Approximately two million marijuana convictions have been expunged or pardoned by states where the drug is now legal, but as many as 30,000 people still sit in prisons across the country, according to the advocacy group the Last Prisoner Project.

People often say the United States is more divided than ever before. Disagreements are regularly simplified to black/white, either/or statements. They are reduced to right and wrong when it is really more accurate to say right and "righter." Our values can often be in competition, even within ourselves.

For example, Alex says he values fairness and hard work. His son has been slacking and barely squeaked out a C– GPA the previous semester. His son failed to apply to other internships on time and wants an internship at Alex's company. Alex leveraged his relationships and position to get the internship for his son.

What happened to the values of fairness and hard work? Is Alex a deceitful hypocrite? Those values didn't go away. They were subordinated to the values of family, loyalty, or legacy. These battles go on within us all the time but we rarely name them.

I believe there is a great benefit to exploring our values and the values of the people we disagree with. By teasing them out and naming the competing values, as well as being intentional around our choices, we can know ourselves better and be more in alignment with what we truly believe.

When you have clarity about your values, making decisions is easier.

TOXIC SUPERSTARS

I once had the managing partner of a prestigious law firm reach out to me to ask if I would agree to coach two of their lawyers. Now in and of itself, this is not a strange request. I work with a number of leaders, CEOs, and managers, who desire to improve their skills in working across difference but I have never been asked to coach lawyers before. Of course I was intrigued to hear more, but was quickly disappointed.

Evidently these two lawyers had participated in a team Zoom happy hour like so many teams held during the COVID-19 pandemic lockdown. The team members were isolated in their homes and had been missing regular interaction, so they were glad to have a chance to kick back and relax, and just have fun with their coworkers. But fun quickly turned into something else. These two lawyers begin to share racist and sexist jokes and comments. Now, one person doing this would have been bad enough, but because they were feeding off of each other, their tirade went on for over twenty minutes. As is so often the case, their coworkers were hesitant to say anything during the call, but they were horrified by what these two lawyers had said and reported them to the leadership team.

Before I say any more, it's important for you to understand that this law firm had no people of color as lawyers in their firm. Not even one out of thirty-five lawyers. And they only had four women, so this is not what you would call a tip-of-the-spear organization when it comes to diversity, equity, and inclusion.

I would have loved to help them with that problem, but that was not the request. The managing partner instead asked me to coach the two attorneys to not be racist. I actually gasped. She wanted me to meet with them once a week to help them understand why diversity is good and why they should be more sensitive.

Lawyers are among the most educated people in our societies. These two men in particular were litigators, which means it was their job to go into courtrooms to persuade other people of a position on behalf of their client. They needed to understand how to talk to people. That was their job. How was it possible that they needed me to explain diversity to them?

Well, she went on to explain. They were both up for partner in the next few months, and the firm wanted to retain them if possible.

Suddenly the picture became clear. These two attorneys were valuable to them, even though they were racist and sexist. They did not see a path to promoting them after such a public display without damaging the morale of the rest of the organization. I was essentially being asked to Blackwash them. To use my credibility to explain away their bad behavior. If they could check a box with me, then they could be promoted without issue.

I'm sure it comes as no surprise to you that I refused this assignment, but I want you to understand why I was deeply offended by it.

First, this organization had no people of color. It had not taken "a risk" on hiring anyone different, but here it was poised to take a risk on two people who have not exhibited even the most basic good judgment to not express racism and sexism on a call with their coworkers. They were in roles that required them to interact frequently with the public at all levels. I wondered how the women on that call felt. The firm was ready to pay a staggering fee to clean up the objectively bad behavior of these two men. What investments had they made in diversifying their firm? None.

The other reason I turned down this assignment is that DEI is not PR. In this case, the teammates on the call were expecting the two attorneys to be fired, definitely not promoted to partner. The managing partner was attempting to use me to spin their very strange decision and sell it to the rest of the organization. I imagine that at the end of our engagement, we would have posed for a picture together in the company newsletter to let everyone know that these two men are OK. That is not what this work is about.

Unfortunately, this firm was not unique in its confusion. Many organizations have confused DEI with public relations, focusing their efforts on external cosmetic work that can easily be listed in the annual shareholders' report, rather than authentic change. The irony that an organization that had little to no diversity itself, outside of the mailroom, would attempt to use DEI to save actors from termination was peak performative DEI.

I passed on that opportunity because I understand the harm toxic superstars do to the growth and maturation of Indivisible teams. You cannot encourage inclusion while actively elevating those who disrespect and sabotage it. Accepting bad behavior is the same as condoning it.

The managing director did not want an Indivisible team. What she wanted was a sanitized performance. That is not what I do, and it's not what you should do either.

BEAUTIFUL BYSTANDERS

After closing a big deal for their company, a group of coworkers went out to celebrate at a local restaurant. They had been putting in lots of late nights, so they were thrilled to finally have this in their rearview mirror. They had earned a delicious dinner.

After a few drinks, Tyler got up to use the restroom. He was at the far end of the table, so most people didn't notice that he was gone. At the other end of the table, Daniel was telling a story about something that had happened in the course of the deal and sought to get Tyler's input on the story. When he didn't see him, he said, "Where is Tyler? Where did our little Niglet go?"

Everyone at the table froze, shifting in their seats uncomfortably. They found excuses to look at their phone or to dig something out of their purse. As you have likely figured out by now, Tyler was the only Black member of the team, and in his absence, not one employee spoke for him. There was another guest at the table, though. The girlfriend of one of the other employees, who also happened to be Black. She waited agonizingly for someone to speak up. She searched their faces for the courage of conviction and was disappointed to see none. Eventually, she could no longer hold her peace.

"Since no one else seems to have an issue with what was just said, I'll speak up." She turned to Daniel and said, "What you just said was completely inappropriate and offensive and I don't know why you'd be so comfortable saying something so racist at the dinner table."

Daniel fumbled through a lukewarm apology and then the group went back to dinner.

Imagine her surprise when, the next day, she received feedback that the employees thought *she* had ruined the dinner. According to them, *she* had been impolite. While they didn't like Daniel's "joke," they thought it was in poor taste to call him out at the table even though he said it at the table. Although she was the only Black person at the table at the time, they got to decide the appropriateness of the reaction to a radicalized insult. They were particularly offended by her assumption that no one else had an issue with what Daniel said.

To be fair, they disliked what he said. But they were more concerned that their silence was misunderstood. They just didn't feel like it was polite to call him out. Even her boyfriend did not speak up. His justification? "I was going to pull him to the side later. I didn't want to make a scene." From her perspective, the scene had already been made. Imagine having a system of mores that penalizes the person who points out offense more than the actual perpetrator of offense.

I don't have to imagine. I see it in every office with almost every client—bad behavior going unchecked because of an inappropriate boundary about what is considered gentile or appropriate. Politeness is strangling our ability to create spaces where everyone feels welcome. It confuses us about who the bad actors are and what our responsibility is toward change. Your culture is defined by what you allow, not just what you do. And when we have been conditioned to turn a blind eye to bad behavior under the guise of decorum, we normalize toxicity.

Chapter 17

Make It Right

*"We have to consciously study how to be tender
with each other until it becomes a habit."*

—AUDRE LORDE

I WAS CONDUCTING A PROJECT FOR A FINANCIAL SERVICES CLIENT. They had an employee, David, who made an incredibly insensitive comment at work. David had offended many people, and the recovery process had not gone well. Our paths crossed during my consultancy with the client, and David approached me for my advice on what was becoming an ugly situation.

In his explanation, David admitted that he was wrong, but unfortunately when talking to his coworkers, he did what so many do. Instead of apologizing, he doubled down.

"I'm sick of cancel culture," he said. "People need to learn to let stuff go. I mean, how long are they gonna be mad about this?"

It's a familiar problem. Sometimes people grow impatient. They demand forgiveness and understanding on their timeline.

"When you call it 'cancel culture,'" I said, "you deflect responsibility. What you said was incredibly disrespectful, but for some reason, you have decided that you get to decide when others should be over it."

As we were sitting and talking, I got a news alert on my phone about Kelley Williams-Bolar, the Black woman who was sent to jail for enrolling her child in a great public school using her father's address. She essentially went to jail for stealing math and dodgeball.

I shared the story with David and was stunned by his response. "Well, she shouldn't have done that. It's not right to lie to get into a better school."

In light of our prior conversation, I was stunned. David had given every reason why his infraction was not that bad, why the punishment had been too severe, and why the victims of his admitted harm were taking it way too far for way too long.

David was clear on the mercy and forgiveness he deserved for causing harm to others but could not find any grace or understanding for a woman who not only had not harmed anyone but did what she did to give her child a chance at a decent education.

I pointed this out to David and he fell quiet. It had never occurred to him how harsh he was to others while craving understanding for himself.

At one point or another in our lives, we have all been David. David illustrates the moving parts of redemption. Fall down, get up, let people up.

FALL DOWN

"She is so angry with me. I don't know what I was thinking. I didn't mean to upset her, but she is furious!"

I can't tell you how many times I've heard a version of this statement. People, in good faith, do or say something that deeply offends another person. Sometimes they are in tears as they share their deep concern that the person they've offended hates them now and they'll never be able to repair the relationship.

Fear of finding oneself in this position immobilizes people. Just one experience is enough to make anyone overly cautious about offending others. While this may seem OK at first glance—we love that people are being thoughtful and have no desire to create harm—this pussyfooting around actually hinders progress. If you don't try, you don't grow. And without growth, we are stuck with what we all agree is a suboptimal status quo.

Anything worth doing is worth failing at. You are going to make mistakes. You will occasionally put your foot in your mouth. There will be times when you will zig when you should have zagged. Accepting that is a critically important part of the journey to being Indivisible. Knowing how to budget for failure and to leave room for missteps is key to moving forward.

Now, to all the perfectionists out there, this may sound sacrilegious. But let me make this clear to you: This is a test where no one gets an A. We all stumble. We all fall short. I've seen so many people eat themselves alive with guilt and shame, which, in my opinion, is wasted energy. People beat themselves up instead of taking the opportunity to grow.

But you deserve to grow. Let yourself. You are under no obligation to be the same person you were a year, month, or even fifteen minutes ago. You can evolve. One of the cornerstones of being Indivisible is being compassionate, but if your compassion doesn't include yourself, it is incomplete. Learn from your mistakes and do better next time.

GET UP

When you do make a mistake, it's important to take responsibility. How do you do that?

The first thing you have to do is apologize. There are a number of ways to think about apology, but my favorite is the four-part apology.

The anatomy is simple:
- Part 1: I'm sorry for . . .
- Part 2: This is wrong because . . .
- Part 3: In the future, I will . . .
- Part 4: Will you forgive me?

In part 1, we have the acknowledgement of the harm. It's important to be clear about the behaviors you are apologizing for.

In part 2, we have the architecture of the offense. By clearly communicating what was harmful about the behavior, you make it clear that you understand exactly what was damaging about it.

In part 3, we detail the plan for the future and what will be different going forward. This element is important because it communicates that there has been some thought about how your behavior needs to change and how it will be different in the future.

In part 4, there is the request for acceptance. Unfortunately, many people skip this step, but in my opinion, it's one of the most important parts of an apology. It clearly communicates the understanding that acceptance is not presumed but humbly requested. By taking the step of asking for forgiveness, we are saying, "I don't just want to end the conflict. I want to restore the relationship."

Let's apply this model to an example. Carrie and Evan have worked together in the accounting department for the last two years but have offices in different parts of the country. Their team gathered for an all-hands retreat at the home office. Carrie is currently eight months pregnant, and when Evan saw her, he reached out and rubbed both hands on her belly through her shirt. "I'm going to have a great year! It's good luck to rub a pregnant woman's belly."

Now, as you can imagine, Carrie was furious. Evan had violated her personal space in a way that would be clearly inappropriate in almost any other context. For example, she could never walk up to someone and rub their bald head. Carrie stormed off, visibly upset, and Evan realized he had clearly used poor judgment.

Evan thinks highly of Carrie and definitely wanted to make amends, so he approached her and offered this apology:

I'm sorry I violated your personal space and touched you without your permission.

This is wrong because I have boundaries I wouldn't want crossed, especially at work. I realize I violated one of yours in an inappropriate way.

In the future, I will keep my hands to myself and not touch people without their permission.

Do you accept my apology? My relationship with you is very important to me and I hate to think that I have damaged it. I hope we can move past this.

I believe that the fourth step is critical and shouldn't be implied. If you don't include the request for forgiveness, you have only listed facts, not humbled yourself to the other person. When you don't offer the "Will you forgive me?" it subtly communicates that there is an expectation that your apology must be accepted.

The more powerful you are, the harder it can be to do the fourth step. Think about how often your parents asked for your forgiveness.

Common Mistakes

You speak about the receiver's reaction instead of your own behavior: Stop saying things like "I'm sorry you feel this way." Apologize for your own behavior, not their reaction.

You make the apology conditional:"I'm sorry IF you were hurt by what I did." That is a toxic "if." If you don't believe you've done anything harmful, why are you apologizing? A better approach would be "I'm unclear about how my actions harmed you, but it is obvious to me that you are upset. Could you please help me understand where I caused offense?" Don't give them an apology you don't feel. If you don't feel it, they won't feel it. Caveat: Some people may have zero interest in explaining it to you. You have to accept that. It's not their job to explain your behavior to you.

You make the apology about you: An apology that requires the receiver to comfort you instead of processing the harm done to them is an epic fail. A heartfelt sincere apology is wonderful. An overly emotional, self-indulgent apology is almost as bad as no apology at all. Manage your emotions and keep the focus on the person you're offering the apology to.

You demand the swift acceptance of your apology: People have a right to heal at their own pace. Their timing isn't up to you. Your job is to offer the apology, not enforce it. The timing you select to offer the apology is up to you. The timing of the acceptance is not.

You minimize the harm: "You know I didn't mean that." "You know I was just joking." "I only did it once." Excuses and justifications are not helpful. When you minimize or excuse the harm, you minimize the efficacy of the apology.

You withhold restitution when it is appropriate: If I borrow your car without your permission and get into a minor accident, it isn't enough to just say "I'm sorry." I also need to offer to pay for the repairs or refill the gas tank.

THE COURAGE TO CORRECT

Restitution is an integral part of being Indivisible. Harm created must be harm corrected.

Consider the decade-long practice of race-norming in the NFL.

In 2013, the NFL began paying players who showed signs of cognitive decline due to playing football. To receive the compensation, players had to be tested by a neuropsychologist and show signs that their mental abilities were failing. The test given included a racial correction.

Race-norming made it more difficult for Black NFL players to receive compensation for dementia caused by football injuries because Black players were automatically assumed to have lower cognitive scores than White players. That made it harder for Black players to show mental decline and led to their receiving compensation less often than non-Black players. In 2021, the NFL agreed to end race-norming in a $1 billion concussion settlement.[69]

If I tell you the NFL leadership identified this heinous racist practice themselves and voluntarily elected to eliminate it, how would you feel? But what if I tell you the NFL was compelled by the court to end the practice? That they hid the data, delayed payments, and fought in court for years to maintain the practice? Does that feel different?

Sincere, intentional restitution is essential if we are to move forward. When you see harm, fix it.

LET OTHER PEOPLE UP

In many places in the country, fires are fought by people incarcerated in our prisons. Nowhere is this truer than in California, where wildfires ravage the state annually. Thousands of incarcerated firefighters compose up to 30 percent of California's woodland firefighting crews. Some of these prisoners fight fires for years before being released from incarceration, but upon release, they have no path to becoming full-time firefighters. They are allowed to be full-time volunteer firefighters for a salary of $8,800 per year, but prohibited from being full-time professional firefighters for a salary of $90,000 per year.[70]

This strikes me as odd.

The goal of the penal system, theoretically, is to rehabilitate offenders, punish them for their infractions, then free them, allowing them to return to society. But, as the national recidivism rate of 41 percent indicates, many are unable to successfully find their footing once they leave prison.[71]

There are a number of reasons this happens:
- The stigma attached to having been imprisoned makes it difficult to reintegrate into society, e.g., finding a job.
- There may be an association with peers involved in criminal activity.
- Inadequate skills necessary for employment.
- Drug or alcohol addiction.
- People are released into the same communities they came from, which may have blight, failing schools, and high unemployment.
- Prison does not address the psychological problems that caused prisoners to commit crimes in the first place, e.g., poor moral development, attribution biases, or mental health issues.

- For a small percentage, prison is preferable to the life they left behind: they have companionship, food, and a warm shelter.

As the country with the largest number of incarcerated citizens by far, this reentry challenge is a crisis of exponential proportions.

The United States has a problem. That's why the California policy is so odd to me. It seems like all the ingredients for an effective solution are present. You take a troubled population that generally has experienced substandard education/training gaps (the average inmate has an eighth-grade education or less). That population is then trained in a much-needed skill at great benefit and little cost to the state of California. Inmates are paid between $2.90 and $5.12 per day to fight fires, sometimes for years.[72] Then it would seem logical that, upon release, those interested in continuing firefighting would be considered trained, tested known quantities who could step right into a profession that provides a great service to the state as well as an income that significantly reduces the chance of that person returning to prison. Everybody wins, right?

Wrong.

1 out of 5 prisoners in the world is incarcerated in the United States

Eleven million people around the world are in prisons and jails. The United States locks up a larger share of these people than any other country, with as many prisoners as the 194 countries with the smallest incarcerated populations combined.

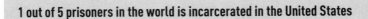

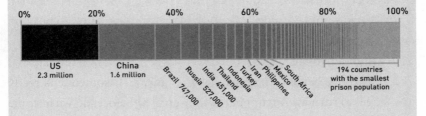

| US 2.3 million | China 1.6 million | Brazil 747,000 | Russia 527,000 | India 451,000 | Thailand | Indonesia | Turkey | Iran | Philippines | Mexico | South Africa | 194 countries with the smallest prison population |

Sources: US incarcerated population from Prison Policy Initiative, Mass Incarceration: The Whole Pie 2019, *and all other data from Institute for Crime & Justice Policy Research,* World Prison Brief *downloaded January 2020.*

Formerly incarcerated people are only allowed to work as a volunteer firefighter. There aren't many places in the United States where an adult person can live on the $8,800 per year volunteer firefighting pays.

This begs a very ugly question: Do we want people to be reformed? Do we want them to return to society after incarceration? Do we want to let them up?

It's no secret that the 13th Amendment, while freeing the majority of enslaved people allowed for one carve out for legal slavery—the compelled free labor of incarcerated people.

Some of the companies that have used prison slave labor at some point in the last twenty-five years would surprise you. They are some of the most beloved brands. You may want to investigate the brands you use to see if prison labor is a part of their supply chain.

The average wage nationwide for incarcerated workers who maintain prison facilities ranges from 13 cents to 52 cents an hour, according to the ACLU and Global Human Rights Clinic.

Unfortunately, we have built whole industries and economies around prison labor. In 2021, Arizona Department of Corrections director David Shinn said Arizona communities would "collapse" without cheap prison labor, during testimony before the Joint Legislative Budget Committee.[73] "There are services that this department provides to city, county, and local jurisdictions that simply can't be quantified at a rate that most jurisdictions could ever afford. If you were to remove these folks from that equation, things would collapse in many of your counties, for your constituents."

In other words, we need to put more people in jail. Imagine that. Most people would consider a dwindling prison population to be good news, but we have whole systems based on not letting people up.

What about you? Do you let people change? Do you let them grow? Can they move beyond the mistakes they make? If someone is ready to change, to turn away from harm they created before, do we become their cage? All too often, we want a grace and mercy for ourselves that we do not extend to others.

Fall down, get up, let people up.

HOW TO MAKE IT LAST/ MAINTAINING THE POWER OF POSSIBILITY

*"Everything now, we must assume, is on our hands:
we have no right to assume otherwise."*

—JAMES BALDWIN

I AM EXCITED. WHEN I THINK ABOUT HOW FAR WE HAVE COME, AND the world we have created thus far, I am encouraged, empowered, and, most importantly, I am catalyzed. It is our turn to write the next chapter. Our privilege to take the next leap forward.

We are powerful people, and we are capable of doing hard things. We sent people to the moon in a tin can using computers not as sophisticated as the phones we carry around in our pockets.

When we work together, we are phenomenal.

Being Indivisible is no easy feat. It will require dedication and the willingness to stumble, get up, and try again. We need to clarify what it means to be a patriot. That word has come to mean too many things in recent years. It isn't about finding hundreds of ways to fashion the American flag into articles of clothing or whether you stand during the anthem. It's about how much you care about others, and how much you invest in future generations. It isn't walking around saying "We're number one." It's working every day to make it so. A patriot loves their country enough to commit to its growth, not just extract from its bounty. Patriotism is not about bursts of energy, but of consistent embodiment of values and ideals. It is a journey.

How do you take the first step on a long journey? Benjamin Franklin famously said, "All mankind is divided into three classes: those that are immovable, those that are moveable, and those that move."

You are a mover. And you're not alone. There are people all around you who believe in the power we all have at our fingertips and who are eager to step into the very important work of being Indivisible. We must not be distracted by those who seek to conflate difference with division. Those whose imaginations are too small to envision what we will become. The loudest voices are not always the strongest.

I believe we have much to celebrate, and we must remember to do so. Big wins, small advancements. All of it. Optimism lubricates the gears of indivisibility.

We must reexamine what it means to be patriotic. Helping others, and ourselves, live out the promise of America is an essential component.

This country is not frail or fragile. We are strong enough to be refined. Resilient enough to be improved. Too many have refused to imagine that we can love our country while working optimistically to repair it. Instead, some have been enlisted as keepers of its myths.

But not you. If you have made it to the end of this book, I know you too have made the commitment to be Indivisible. I thank you in advance for the changes you will make in your world. I know sometimes you will be afraid to say or do the wrong thing. And sometimes you will get it wrong. But I trust I have said something that will encourage you to do it anyway.

I believe in you.

Now the work begins.

INDIVISIBLE AT WORK

T HERE HAVE BEEN MANY CONCEPTS AND IDEAS SHARED IN THIS book and if you've made it this far, you are clearly committed to incorporating some of them into your life. To that end, this appendix contains several practical applications for your consideration.

The average working adult spends 90,000 hours of their life on the job.[74] Figuring out ways to effectively work with coworkers, customers, stakeholders, and leaders is a critical skill. This section contains several exercises that will help you do that.

TO WHOM IT SHOULD CONCERN

One of the biggest challenges of being truly Indivisible is the idea that it requires the involvement of everyone. Once you decide that deep change is required, it is up to you to involve as many stakeholders at as many different points of the organization as possible in the effort. But there's a problem. Everybody wants to change the world. Very few people want to change themselves.

So how do you set the stage for change? Whether you are trying to create an Indivisible company, business unit, sports team, or family, the following process creates a powerful framework for change.

- Communicate the need for change clearly and transparently, involving all concerned parties in the change process.
- Model the desired behaviors and attitudes through leadership actions and decisions.
- Encourage open communication and feedback from the team. Address concerns and answer questions about the change. Debunk any misconceptions.
- "Feed the canaries." All too often, we punish people who identify problems instead of using them as a valuable indicator of flaws or constraints to our proposed solutions.
- Align systems, policies, and practices with the desired culture. Cultural change does not happen in isolation. It must be embodied by all the appropriate systems within the context. Anything else reads as hypocrisy.
- Provide resources and support to help team members adapt to the change, especially training and development opportunities to help employees develop new skills. Don't assume everyone has the skills to execute the changes you want to create. Teach them.
- Empower each individual to take responsibility for the change. Emphasize the team's strengths and how they can be leveraged during the change process.

- Encourage team members to take ownership of their role in the change process. Build a coalition of support, and involve everyone in decision-making as much as possible.
- Celebrate success and recognize the effort made by team members during the change. Recognize and encourage the people who embody the desired culture.
- Continuously reassess and adjust the change plan as needed, based on team feedback and organizational performance. Continuously reinforce the desired culture through ongoing communication and recognition.
- Stay open and flexible to changing the plan, if necessary, to address resistance and minimize its impact.

Every system has inputs, throughputs, and outputs. It is very easy to focus our attention solely on the outcomes. We can metaphorically spend all of our time cleaning up spider webs, or we can take on the critical work of catching the spider. The murder of George Floyd is a perfect example. If emergency medical services had arrived eight minutes into the attack and revived him, we would never have heard George Floyd's name. George Floyd's death was a tragedy, but his death shouldn't be required for us to be horrified by the process. You don't have to be a hashtag to be terrorized. We were horrified by the outcome, but the outcome is a web, not the spider. It's the process we must reckon with. Are we focusing on the process or just living a whack-a-mole existence responding to tragedy? We must have the courage to find the root causes of harm. We must kill the spider.

Everybody wants to change the world, but nobody wants to change their world.

WHO'S ON YOUR TEAM

Sometimes when we talk about issues of diversity, people define these historical issues, but, in my experience, we get much further if we are able to challenge ourselves to ask the hard questions about our personal interactions with diversity today. How much difference is there in our lives? Where does it show up? How is it treated?

You can read all the books in the world (and I'm super glad you're reading this one), but nothing changes until you interrogate your own beliefs.

Consider the following questions:
- Have you ever had a woman as a boss? How do you think women lead differently from men?
- Should people lose their jobs because they are caught in racist behavior? What should the consequences be for acts of overt racism? When does it go too far?
- How do you think about members of your family who have deeply bigoted views? Do you stay in relationship with them? Attempt to change their mind? Avoid the topic altogether?
- What preconceived notions do you have about the ways other religions practice?

THE ALL HANDS POLICY CHECK

One of the ways we can evaluate our decisions with a wider lens is to conduct an all-hands policy check. This four-step process allows for a deeper evaluation of ideas to determine their efficacy across different impacted groups.

The process is as follows:
1. Create idea
2. Determine stakeholders (each discrete)
3. Assess impact on each group
4. Refine policy

Let's work through this framework with four examples.

Men's Dress Shirts

When I worked in the commercial real estate industry, there were very few female brokers. One of the landlords offered an incentive to brokers who placed a certain level of tenants in their buildings: a custom-made dress shirt.

Create idea	Give brokers a custom-made men's dress shirt as an incentive gift.
Determine stakeholders	Brokers: 85% men; 15% women Age 25–35: 30%; age 35–45: 55%; age 46+: 15%.
Assess impact	Most men will appreciate a custom-made men's dress shirt, regardless of age or income. Most women will not appreciate a custom-made men's dress shirt.
Refine policy	Create an alternate gift for women brokers.

Without this process, thoughtlessness can make you miss your target.

PTO

Vacation and sick time are blended into one category of time off called "PTO," with limitations on how much PTO can be rolled over from year to year. The impact of this if you are twenty-five, single, and healthy is relatively minimal. If you are older, married, have children, care for sick parents, or have any health problems, this practice is extremely harmful to you because your preference might be to roll over this time in the event that you or a loved one would have the caregiving responsibility for experiences a health emergency. This impacts women in the sandwich generation more than any other group.

Create idea	Merge sick days and vacation days into one bank of paid time off.
Determine stakeholders	50% have children; 30% have aging parents; 22% have a chronic illness; 61% of women are caregivers for someone else.
Assess impact	Single, healthy employees who are not caregivers have less demand on sick time. Those with young children or chronic illnesses are more likely to need sick days to care for themselves or a loved one. Combining PTO would leave many without vacation time. If rolling over/saving time isn't allowed, older or chronically ill employees, who may be prone to more serious illnesses that require more time off, would not be able to budget sick time for future use.
Refine policy	Keep vacation and sick time separate or offer option to pool.

Serious cracks can appear when you don't consider edge cases and the unique needs of your different constituency groups.

Turkey Trot

On Thanksgiving Day, a 5K run is set up so that community members can do a group workout experience before they eat a large meal.

Create idea	Host a Turkey Trot to get community members active and raise money for charity.
Determine stakeholders	Middle-aged men and women; senior citizens; children.
Assess impact	Women especially may be preparing Thanksgiving dinner during selected time slot. Senior citizens may be physically unable to participate. Younger children may be unable to keep up/may need to ride in a stroller.
Refine policy	Accept exclusion of a group/groups, or move event to a later time when more people can participate.

You don't have to change your plan. You can't always accommodate everyone. The key is to be intentional. If you do exclude a population from an event or program, e.g., a women's retreat or a men's prayer breakfast, it's important to do it thoughtfully and to balance your other offerings to intentionally include other groups when appropriate.

Holiday Party

A team wants to host their holiday party at an all-you-can-eat Brazilian steakhouse.

Create idea	Host a holiday party at a steakhouse to show employees our appreciation.
Determine stakeholders	80% eat meat; 15% are vegetarian; 5% are vegan.
Assess impact	Vegetarians and vegans won't be able to eat the restaurant's main food.
Refine policy	Call the restaurant. They offer vegetarians and vegan options! We can continue with the original idea.

A little fact-finding goes a long way toward ensuring the needs of each team member are acknowledged. It's a special touch to include these findings in the invitation so that vegetarians would know they were considered from the outset, not as an afterthought.

Taking the time to conduct a simple analysis can help you avoid inadvertent missteps. Even when policies are not changed, people generally appreciate that they were considered and not thoughtlessly overlooked.

PACE YOURSELF

I have a special soft spot for middle managers. Managers today report higher levels of stress and burnout. Because of this, they are leaving their jobs at higher rates than non-managers.

It may sound strange coming from me, but it is possible to do too much. There are many times I have gone into organizations that are completely overburdened with initiatives and programs. Businesses must continue to work on many big challenges, but there must be coordination. Sometimes I present to a company or business unit and I can tell the employees are not resistant to DEI, they are resistant to "one more thing." We cannot allow fatigue and overwhelm to rob us of the opportunity to create Indivisible teams.

Here are solutions I help organizations implement:

Conduct an initiative audit: Organizations should document the many tasks and initiatives they now expect middle managers to engage in. Have managers themselves provide this information, and create a spreadsheet. Many managers are so used to their mega-load of responsibilities that they take some for granted, so it's important to encourage all managers to thoughtfully weigh in. Together, they can make sure everything is listed.

Find the overlaps: When executives see all this listed, many realize it is too much for anyone to handle. They may also realize something very helpful: There are overlaps among different initiatives. For example, the company may have managers overseeing a peer coaching program to help employees gain new skills, while also having a separate program to help employees build one-on-one relationships, which are crucial for engagement. However, peer coaching can do both, so a separate program may not be needed.

Edit strategically: Because I work so hard to advance DEI in organizations, executives are often surprised when I say they should put off some of their initiatives. But some of the programs and events on their dockets—such as full-day training sessions once a month, for example—add even more work for managers and create more resentment than advancement. It's far more damaging for organizations to exhaust managers to the breaking point. I've found that a great many managers are genuinely committed to important goals such as DEI.

The problem is not psychological resistance; it's fatigue. When managers who share these values leave the company, they take all their work and knowledge with them—setting back these efforts.

Consider expanding middle management: Traditionally, middle management has gotten a bad rap. Many people have seen large ranks of middle managers as being a sign that a company is too bloated. Yahoo reported in 2019 that "companies are beginning to change this structure by cutting down layers of management in an attempt to streamline business and cut down on unnecessary costs." But since then, the work of middle managers has revolutionized. With everything managers are now expected to do, giving them smaller teams to oversee can sometimes be a very helpful part of the solution. And that means hiring more managers, to reduce the ratio.

While all these steps will help, it's also crucial to listen to managers about what would work best for them. Ask them how they're doing, what resources they need, and what changes would help. Perhaps hold an off-site event for them, in which they are honored and given a chance to brainstorm about how to make their work lives better. Managers want to be part of the solution—they just need a chance to breathe.

ANNUAL INDIVISIBLE PLANNING

Being Indivisible is not an event. It is a way of life that must be activated on a consistent basis. Whether you run a company, sports team, school, or household, you should have an intentional plan to grow.

It can be tempting to think of this work in bursts of energy, but it is far more effective to build intentionality around regular, consistent improvement.

One approach is to think of your commitment across several dimensions on an annual basis. The four areas are understanding, skills, actions, and systems. What activities do you plan to engage in for the next twelve months? Be as concrete and specific as possible and make sure there are activities in each quadrant.

Being Indivisible is not an event, it is a practice. By committing to growing throughout the year, you secure growth for a lifetime.

	Understanding	Skills	Actions	Systems
Q1	Watch a documentary about the Chinese Exclusion Act.	Ask Linda to work with me to revise the housing policy.	Host junior women for a Q&A to learn how they are growing in the company.	Review job descriptions to select which ones should not require a degree.
Q2	Attend an event hosted by an ERG in my company.	Meet Thomas for lunch to work on communicating more effectively with him.	Review charitable donations. What new charities should I consider?	Figure out how to support more women running for office.
Q3	Watch *13th* and *When They See Us.*	Work on listening skills: Schedule 5 conversations; commit to doing no more than 40% of the talking.	Attend a worship service of a different denomination.	Review the fees I am paying to service providers. Are they fair? Equitable?
Q4	Watch the TED Talk "The Danger of a Single Story" by Chimamanda Ngozi Adichie.	Learn better mediation practices.	Select a new accountant. Ask friends for suggestions for people of color.	Review company holiday policies. Are we inclusive of other faiths?

HOW TO EVALUATE SYSTEMS

When evaluating the systems you engage with, it might be helpful to conduct a process evaluation: List the steps involved in your key processes. Then create six to eight fictitious case studies to move through the process, assessing areas of friction or decreased opportunity.

Examples of avatars could be:
- Linda, 60: Recently widowed Black woman with thirty years of experience in the field. Petite and soft-spoken.
- Maria, 24: Hispanic student from a local college, who has no internships or extracurriculars and who worked her way through school.
- Brandon, 37: Disabled Asian man unable to physically come to the office.
- Rick, 42: White Veteran with a service animal.
- Claudia, 35: White single mother to twin boys.

In this exercise, you might be tempted to focus on recruitment or onboarding. Those processes are important, but to conduct an accurate assessment of your culture, one must examine the deeper processes: holiday parties, promotions, employee retreats, group projects, meetings. By doing this, you will be able to identify areas of opportunity to be more inclusive.

For example, do you have to have the morning meeting at 7:30 a.m., which may be difficult for parents doing school drop-off, or could you have it at 8:15, when everyone can easily attend? Do PTA meetings have to happen at ten in the morning, when working parents are unavailable to participate? Taking the time to look at the systems we operate in and adjust them where necessary is challenging but important work.

The Tool Kit

INDIVISIBLE EVERYDAY

WHETHER YOU'RE A LITTLE LEAGUE COACH, BOOK CLUB LEADER, or Sunday school teacher, we all have the power to be impactful. And we should use it. This section offers up a few ways to consider the world around us in order to identify places where our voices and our hands are needed.

Thank you for your willingness to do the work. It matters.

WHO WE'RE WATCHING

As an executive who always navigated predominantly White spaces, I had to know *Seinfeld* and *Friends* jokes to fit in. I had to watch *The Office* to be relatable. I've always marveled at how little energy people from other groups have put into learning about me.

Are you curious about other cultures? Do you seek out information about the people who work for you and with you? Where do you get your information about their stories? If you only watch your stories, how are you ever going to be able to incorporate the stories of others? When the hero of every story from Luke Skywalker to Frodo looks the same, it's hard to imagine anyone else in that role. There's something about entertainment that's really powerful. You can devote two hours of your life to immersing yourself in someone else's experience. It's an entertaining (and relatively painless) way to grow in your understanding.

I have a list of such stories, most of which are award-winning movies. I've been sharing them with executives all over the country to see how many they've personally seen. The results have been fascinating. Most have seen fewer than five from a list of 150. Some of these movies and TV shows are over thirty years old, which means there has been ample opportunity to see them, just no interest.

Whose stories are you watching? The following is a list of critically acclaimed movies and TV shows that center on the experiences of diverse populations.

How many of these have you seen?

- *Glory*
- *Special*
- *Slumdog Millionaire*
- *Speechless*
- *Parasite*
- *Soul Surfer*
- *Abbott Elementary*
- *Moonlight*
- *Crazy Rich Asians*
- *Get Out*
- *Breaking Fast*
- *Dorothy Dandridge*
- *Bombshell*
- *Fresh Off the Boat*
- *Mo*
- *Ugly Betty*
- *Killing Eve*
- *Watchmen*
- *Everything Everywhere All at Once*
- *West Side Story*
- *School Ties*
- *Black Panther*
- *On My Block*
- *Gandhi*
- *Paris Is Burning*
- *Wonder*
- *Always Be My Maybe*
- *Pan's Labyrinth*
- *Crip Camp*
- *King Richard*
- *Minari*
- *Coco*
- *The Intern*
- *Spirited Away*
- *Atypical*
- *Judas and the Black Messiah*
- *Shang-Chi and the Legend of the Ten Rings*
- *Lovecraft Country*

- *One Day at a Time*
- *Jane the Virgin*
- *The Kite Runner*
- *Still Alice*
- *Milk*
- *Dream Girls*
- *Ray*
- *Squid Game*
- *In the Heights*
- *Love, Simon*
- *Lion*
- *Harriet*
- *Woman King*
- *Frida*
- *On the Basis of Sex*
- *City of God*
- *Brokeback Mountain*

- *Hidden Figures*
- *Life of Pi*
- *13th*
- *A Time to Kill*
- *Kim's Convenience*
- *I Am Sam*
- *The Farewell*
- *The King and I*
- *The White Tiger*
- *She Said*
- *1923*
- *Ramy*
- *Joy*
- *RuPaul's Drag Race*
- *Loving*
- *Nora from Queens*

ASK YOURSELF HARD QUESTIONS

Many of us think of ourselves as inclusive or color-blind in a broad societal sense, but I'd like to challenge us to think about the ways our values play out in our daily lives. One place this seems to manifest is in the service providers we select to help advance our lives. When it's up to you, who do you choose?

These service providers are segmented into two groups: Thought partners and physical partners. In this exercise, I invite you to indicate which partners are White and which are non-White.

Thought Partners	White	Non-White
Doctor		
Lawyer		
Accountant		
Dentist		
Insurance agent		
Financial planner		
Architect		
Realtor		
Physical Partners		
Housekeeper		
Lawn services		
Manicurist		
Pool services		
Nanny/childcare		
Plumber		

THE GOOD GIVERS TOOLKIT

Traditional holiday toy drives for the poor often involve a Santa Claus figure distributing gifts to children while their parents watch from the sidelines. However, this approach can sometimes diminish the parents' role instead of preserving the dignity and agency of parents in low-income communities. This toolkit introduces an alternative model called "the Good Givers," which aims to shift the focus away from the giver and empower parents in low-income communities. This annual toy giveaway prioritizes the needs and preferences of the children and ensures that the parents play an active role in selecting gifts for their families. They know their children better than you do and this allows them to provide for their children, instead of strangers acting as heroes in their children's lives.

To host your own Good Givers holiday event, download the toolkit at allhandsgrp.com/thegoodgivers.

ACKNOWLEDGMENTS

Everything about the process of writing this book has felt miraculous to me. So many people have opened up their hearts and minds to bring this book to life.

This book would not have happened in this way without the generosity, openness, patience, and advocacy of Adam Grant. There are talkers, promisers, and complimenters, and then there are doers. Adam Grant is a doer, and he has sewn in me a commitment to help others when I am able to.

Another champion in this process has been my literary agent, Christy Fletcher of United Talent Agency. She believed in this first-time author and, with the support of her team, has shepherded me through this process. I am so fortunate to have her on my side.

The amazing team at Countryman Press and W. W. Norton have parsed every word and helped me to make this work clear and even more powerful. My editor, Ann Treistman, has polished and pushed me to possibility. Maya Goldfarb, Devorah Backman, and Zachary Polendo have packaged and positioned this book with the energy and optimism that I needed.

Being new to this process, I sought out the authors around me and they did not disappoint. They shared their best advice, their kind encouragement, and the occasional kick in the butt. Joan Ball, Tara

Jaye Frank, Amy Hertz, Kathryn Finney, Josh Levs, Alexandra Carter, Dr. Tina Opie, Laura Gassner Otting, Rahaf Harfoush, Susan McPherson, Joe Mull, Minda Harts, Jenna Arnold, and Elle Stern. Being surrounded by such genius was more than I could've hoped for.

There are some people who have acted as thought partners for me, examining and challenging the concepts I discuss here, helping me to refine them and often simplify them. Angela Blanchard, Dorothy Toran, Misty Starks, Melissa Hensley, Francesca Hogi, Patrick Washington, Abdul Kamara, Kat Cole, Samira Salman, Ryan Weiss, Trisha Cornwell, Summer Owens, and John Register. There are more I know. Please charge any omissions to my head and not my heart.

Special thanks to my dad, Norman Allen, who was the ultimate beta reader. And to my mom, Penelope Allen, who made me who I am.

My anchor throughout this process has been my husband, Matt, who teaches me every day what an Indivisible Leader looks like. He is kind, supportive, brave, and believes in the potential of every person. I have learned so much from him. He's cute, too.

Lastly, I want to thank my daughter, Javan (pronounced *jay-ven*, she's very particular). I literally could not have delivered this book without her. She was my scribe, my researcher, my head cheerleader, my midnight snack preparer, my driver, my comforter, and occasionally my prison guard. It was truly lovely to work on this book with my personal hero. She has overcome so much, and her strength helped me to finish this first important work and share it with you, the reader. Thank you for the gift of your attention.

NOTES

1. Centers for Disease Control and Prevention, "Working Together to Reduce Black Maternal Mortality," Health Equity, CDC.gov, April 3, 2023.
2. CDC, "Working Together."
3. Maya Salam, "For Serena Williams, Childbirth Was a Harrowing Ordeal. She's Not Alone," *New York Times*, January 17, 2018.
4. Saint Luke's Health System, "KSHB: Suicide Rates High in Middle-Aged White Men," September 21, 2022.
5. Harmeet Kaur, "What Studies Reveal about Gun Ownership in the US," CNN, June 2, 2022.
6. American Sociological Association, "White Men Attach Greater Stigma To Mental Health Care," September 10, 2008, www.sciencedaily.com/releases.
7. Aminah Khan, "Kaplan on High Rate of Suicide among White Men." UCLA Luskin School of Public Affairs, November 16, 2022.
8. "Constitutional Rights Foundation," n.d., www.crf-usa.org/black-history-month/the-constitution-and-slavery.
9. History.com Editors, "Harriet Tubman: Facts, Underground Railroad & Legacy," History.com, last updated March 29, 2023.
10. William M. Etter, "False Teeth," *The Digital Encyclopedia of George Washington*, n.d.
11. Washington Library, "Slave Clothing," *The Digital Encyclopedia of George Washington*, n.d.

12. Carrie Blazina and Drew DeSilver, "House Gets Younger, Senate Gets Older: A Look at the Age and Generation of Lawmakers in the 118th Congress," *Pew Research Center*, January 30, 2023.

13. Rose Heichelbech, "What Was the Most Popular Toy the Year You Were Born?," *Dusty Old Thing*, February 9, 2022.

14. David J. Leonard and Stephanie Troutman Robbins, eds., *Race in American Television: Voices and Visions That Shaped a Nation*, (Westport, CT: Greenwood, 2020).

15. Harry Enten, "Americans See Martin Luther King Jr. as a Hero Now, but That Wasn't the Case during His Lifetime," CNN, January 16, 2023.

16. Jamela Adam, "When Could Women Open a Bank Account?," *Forbes Advisor*, updated March 20, 2023.

17. Press Association, "Tiger Woods Delivers Emotional Speech during Golf Hall of Fame Induction," *The 42*, March 10, 2022.

18. History.com Editors, "Vanessa Williams Becomes First Black Miss America," History.com, last updated September 15, 2020.

19. Anjuli Sastry Krbechek, "When LA Erupted in Anger: A Look Back at the Rodney King Riots," NPR, April 26, 2017.

20. Department of Justice, "Federal Domestic Violence Laws," Issues and Answers, Justice.gov, May 26, 2020.

21. Zoe Williams, "Sex, Power and Humiliation: Eight Lessons Women Learned from Monica Lewinsky's Shaming," *Guardian*, September 30, 2021.

22. Jay L. Hoecker, "Vicks VapoRub: An Effective Nasal Decongestant?," Mayo Clinic, December 7, 2021.

23. Alanna Durkin Richer, "Convictions, Prison Time: A Look at College Admissions Scam," AP News, January 4, 2023.

24. Daniel A. Gross, "How Elite US Schools Give Preference to Wealthy and White 'Legacy' Applicants," *Guardian*, January 23, 2019.

25. Josh Moody, "Where the Top Fortune 500 CEOs Attended College," *US News & World Report*, June 16, 2021.

26. United Negro College Fund, "Audacity to Lead," UNCF, July 6, 2021.

27. Rob Picheta, "Black Newborns More Likely to Die When Looked after by White Doctors," CNN, August 20, 2020.

28. "Nazi Persecution of Jehovah's Witnesses," n.d., encyclopedia.ushmm .org/content/en/article/nazi-persecution-of-jehovahs-witnesses.

29. Michel Martin, "Slave Bible from the 1800s Omitted Key Passages That Could Incite Rebellion," NPR, December 9, 2018.

30. Brigit Katz, "Heavily Abridged 'Slave Bible' Removed Passages That Might Encourage Uprisings," *Smithsonian*, January 4, 2019.

31. Rozina Sini, "Publisher Apologises for 'Racist' Text in Medical Book." *BBC News*, October 20, 2017.

32. Tom Dart, "Textbook Passage Referring to Slaves as 'Workers' Prompts Outcry," *Guardian*, July 14, 2017.

33. Tyler Kingkade, "ACLU Lawsuit Says Oklahoma's Anti-Critical Race Theory Law Violates Free Speech," October 20, 2021.

34. "No, Schools Do Not Have Litter Boxes for Students," October 14, 2022. www.nbcnews.com/tech/misinformation/urban-myth-litter-boxes-schools-became-gop-talking-point-rcna51439.

35. Caitlin O'Kane, "High School Robotics Team Builds Electric Wheelchair for 2-Year-Old Whose Family Couldn't Afford One," CBS News, April 2, 2019.

36. Geoffrey Robertson, "It's Time for Museums to Return Their Stolen Treasures," CNN, June 11, 2020.

37. Graham Bowley, "For US Museums with Looted Art, the Indiana Jones Era Is Over," *New York Times*, December 16, 2022.

38. Euronews, "Three Human Skulls from the Colonial Era Removed from Auction in Belgium," *Euronews*, December 1, 2022.

39. Neil de Grasse Tyson, "The Tidal Force," November 1, 1995, neildegrassetyson.com/essays/1995-11-the-tidal-force.

40. The Canadian Encyclopedia. "Inuktitut Words for Snow and Ice," n.d.

41. Kohrman, Miles. "The World Sent 65,Teddy Bears to Newtown. His Job Was to Keep the Gifts from Overwhelming the Town." *The Trace*, September 10, 2020.

42. US Census Bureau, "Anniversary of Americans With Disabilities Act: July 26, 2021," Census.gov, June 29, 2022.

43. "Unemployment Rate for People with a Disability Declines to 7.3 Percent in 2019: The Economics Daily," US Bureau of Labor Statistics, March 2, 2020.

44. William H. Herman and Shihchen Kuo, "100 Years of Insulin: Why Is Insulin So Expensive and What Can Be Done to Control Its Cost?," *Endocrinology and Metabolism Clinics of North America* 50, no. 3 (September 1, 2021): e21–34.

45. Ramtin Arablouei, "The Complicated Relationship between Puerto Rico and US Mainland," NPR, September 23, 2019.

46. History.com Editors, "US Slavery: Timeline, Figures & Abolition," History.com, April 20, 2021.

47. History.com Editors, "Trail of Tears: Definition, Date & Cherokee Nation," History.com, April 20, 2023.

48. Jone Johnson Lewis, "A Short History of Women's Property Rights in the United States," *ThoughtCo*, July 13, 2019.

49. National Archives, "Chinese Exclusion Act (1882)," Archives.gov, January 17, 2023.

50. History.com Editors, "Japanese Internment Camps: WWII, Life & Conditions," History.com, October 29, 2021.

51. Daniel A Gross, "The US Government Turned Away Thousands of Jewish Refugees, Fearing That They Were Nazi Spies," *Smithsonian*, November 18, 2015.

52. Justin McCarthy, "Same-Sex Marriage Support Inches Up to New High of 71%." Gallup, June 10, 2022.

53. Bryan Pietsch, "Texas High Schoolers Set Prices for Classmates in 'Slave Trade' Chat," *New York Times*, April 14, 2021.

54. Ashley Sharp, "River Valley High Football Players Apologize for Participating in Mock Slave-Auction Video," CBS News, October 18, 2022.

55. ABC7 Chicago, "Teacher, Principal on Leave after Student's Project on Hitler," June 5, 2021.

56. Michael Bamberger, "With One Heartfelt Speech, Tiger Woods Revealed Many New Sides of Himself, Golf.com, March 10, 2022, golf.com/news/speech-tiger-woods-revealed-new-sides.

57. Richard Jean So and Gus Wezerek, "Opinion: Just How White Is the Book Industry?," *New York Times*, December 14, 2020.

58. Michael Levenson, "James Patterson Apologizes for Saying White Writers Face a 'Form of Racism,'" *New York Times*, June 15, 2022.

59. Bureau of Labor Statistics, "Labor Force Participation of Mothers and Fathers Little Changed in 2021, Remains Lower than in 2019," *Economics Daily*, US Department of Labor, April 27, 2022.

60. Kyle Macdonald, "The Time When Joshua Bell Went Busking in the Subway, and No-One Noticed," Classic FM, June 10, 2022.

61. Chris Isidore and Matt Egan, "Wells Fargo CEO Apologizes for Saying the Black Talent Pool Is Limited," CNN, September 23, 2020.

62. Your Black World, "Shocking List of 10 Companies That Profited from the Slave Trade," *Race, Racism and the Law*, August 31, 2013, racism .org/index.php?option=com_content&view=article&id=1697: reparations1001; Hal Clay, "Forty Acres and a Mule: America's Bill for Reparations is Long Past Overdue," *The Scholar: St. Mary's Law Review on Race and Social Justice* 24 (3), 2022, commons.stmarytx.edu/cgi/ viewcontent.cgi?article=1399&context=thescholar.

63. Melanie Hanson, "Average Cost of College Over Time: Yearly Tuition Since 1970," Education Data Initiative, January 9, 2022.

64. RAINN, "Perpetrators of Sexual Violence: Statistics," n.d.

65. Michael Barthel, Amy Mitchell, and Jesse Holcomb, "Many Americans Believe Fake News Is Sowing Confusion," Journalism, Pew Research Center, August 27, 2020.

66. Samantha Kummerer, "A Majority of Police Agencies across the US Increased Budgets Despite 'Defund' Movement," ABC11, October 14, 2022.

67. Sam Levin, " 'It Never Stops': Killings by US Police Reach Record High in 2022," *Guardian*, January 16, 2023.

68. Jeremy Berke and Yeji Jesse Lee., "Top Executives at the 14 Largest Cannabis Companies Are Overwhelmingly White Men, an Insider Analysis Shows," *Business Insider*, June 30, 2021.

69. Associated Press, "NFL Agrees to End Race-Based Brain Testing in $1B Settlement on Concussions," NPR, October 21, 2021.

70. Nick Sibilla, "Federal Judge: Californians Who Fought Fires In Prison Can't Become Career Firefighters," *Forbes*, February 16, 2021.

71. UNC School of Government. "A Look at the 2022 Sentencing Commission Recidivism Report," n.d., www.sog.unc.edu/blogs/nc-criminal -law/look-2022-sentencing-commission-recidivism-report.

72. Kevin Stark, "Coronavirus Pandemic Sidelines California's Inmate Firefighters." *NPR*, July 29, 2020.

73. Jimmy Jenkins, "Arizona Communities Would 'Collapse' without Cheap Prison Labor, Corrections Director Says," *Arizona Republic*, July 15, 2022.

74. FreshBooks, "How Many Hours Does the Average Person Work Per Week?," April 18, 2023, www.freshbooks.com/hub/productivity/how -many-hours-does-the-average-person-work.

INDEX

complex nature of, 13
danger of single, 19
incomplete, 11–15
letting go of broken, 3–20
as outright lies, 16–18
transmission of culture and values
in, 5–6
Strangers, warning children about,
126–127
stranger danger PSAs, 126
Strategic editing, 184–185
Subjectivity of language, 40
Success, celebrating, 179
Suffering as entertainment, 23–25
Systems, 142–144
evaluating, 187

T

Team, diversity of members,
179–180
Tempo, setting the, 85–87
Three-Fifths Compromise, 116–117
Tip-of-the-spear organization, 160
Tolerance, problem with, xvi–xx
Toxicity
adapting to, 158
normalizing, 163
Toxic superstars, 159–161
Trail of Tears, 74, 79
Trust, building, 95
Truth
discerning from fiction, 4
reconciling, 5
Tubman, Harriet, xx–xxiv
Turner, Brock, trial of, 143–144
Turtles
as endangered species, 125–126

impact of artificial lights on,
125–126
Tutu, Desmond, 43
Twain, Mark, 19
Tyson, Neil de Grasse, 31

V

Values, transmission of, in stories,
5–6

W

Washington, George, 18
lack of generosity, 4
as slaveholder, 78–79
story of false teeth, 3–4
Weaponization of language,
34–37
Wells Fargo
finding qualified black leaders at,
105
settlement of discrimination cases
at, 106–107
Scharf, Charles W. (CEO),
105–107
start of, 106
"When I, then I" thinking, 123
White men
socialization of, x–xi
suicide rate of, x, xi
White women, maternal mortality
rate of, 9
Will & Grace, 77
Williams, Serena, pregnancy of, ix
Williams, Vanessa, 6
Williams-Bolar, Kelley, 165
Winfrey, Oprah, 111
Winners-take-all mentality, 67–68